Our Lady's Messages from Naju
Compiled according to subject

Published by
Mary's Touch By Mail

Published by:

Mary's Touch By Mail
P.O. Box 1668
Gresham, OR 97030 U.S.A.

Contents

THE CHURCH AND RECENT REVELATIONS

by Fr. Robert J. Billett, C.M.F.

All through Sacred History we see the intervention of our loving God and Creator who tries to keep us on the straight and narrow path to Heaven, and calls us back when we go astray. Through special persons whom He has chosen, like Abraham, Moses and the Prophets, God has been revealing His truth to us and confirming it with miraculous signs. But also throughout Sacred History, side by side with God's true emissaries, we find the self-appointed false prophets. Discernment between true revelation and false revelation, between true signs and false signs, between Prophets and false ones has always been difficult. But God has always helped His Chosen People of the Old Testament and His Chosen People of the New Testament in His Church to be able to discern whether spirits are good or bad, true or false.

By a decree approved by Pope Paul VI on October 14, 1966, dissemination of information on new revelations, apparitions and miracles has been allowed without prior Church approval, provided that such information does not contain anything contrary to the teachings of the Church. The Church always reserves to herself the final decision regarding the truth or falsity of any revelation. In recent times there seems to have been an explosion of information dealing with allegedly supernatural phenomena. There are two sides to this development.

The Positive Side

On the one hand, many people seem to have benefited spiritually from such information. An awareness of heavenly messages and signs can be a fresh stimulus and powerful encouragement for people to deepen their faith in God and to reform their lives.

That is what happened in ancient times to the people of Nineveh, who repented of their sins because of the preaching of the Prophet Jonah, and thus avoided the threatened chastisement of God.

That is what happened at the time of Jesus who came to redeem us. There were many supernatural revelations and signs attesting to the truth of His Mission and Gospel Messages. Many people heeded the revelations and signs, and believed in Jesus and changed their lives. The Blessed Virgin Mary believed the revelation of the Angel Gabriel regarding the Incarnation of the Son of God, and generously accepted all that this entailed for her. St. Joseph heeded the revelations of the Angel regarding the divine origin of Jesus and regarding the need to flee into Egypt. The Shepherds believed the revelation of the Angels regarding the Birth of Jesus Christ. The Wise Men heeded the supernatural sign that led them toward Bethlehem to adore Jesus. The Apostles' faith in Jesus was confirmed by Jesus' miracle at Cana. Jesus Himself appealed to His miraculous works as proof of the truth of His divine words.

And this stimulus of revelations and miracles has continued all through the Christian era.

That is what happened at Guadalupe in 1531, when the people accepted the miraculous image of Our Lady on Juan Diego's tilma as a sign from God and they cast aside idolatry and embraced the Catholic Faith. That too is what so often happens when people read the lives of the Saints, many of whom were blessed with apparitions of Our Lord or Our Lady, with miraculous healings, with the Stigmata, and other supernatural phenomena. By knowledge of such events in the lives of the Saints and their examples of profound love for God and neighbors and self-denial, people are often moved to repentance, conversion, amendment and sanctification.

The Negative Side

On the other hand, the proliferation of information about new revelations has resulted in some confusion and has led to two extremes.

(a) At one extreme, there are people who reject all reported revelations. Of these, some will not accept revelations until they are officially approved by the Church. It is certainly commendable that people follow the Church. But the Church allows people to accept revelations which are not contrary to the teachings of the Church, but always with the proviso that people will abide by the final decision of the Church. The Church is always slow and cautious in the case of private revelations, because we already have in the Deposit of Faith everything necessary for salvation.

(b) At the other extreme, there are people who tend to accept anything and everything when it comes to revelations and apparitions. Where there is such a lack of discrimination and discernment, people run the risk of putting themselves above the Church and her Magisterium. With that decree of 1966 the Holy Father did not relinquish the Church's authority. It is still true that the final decision about the truth or falsity of any revelations remains the prerogative of the Church, which has been so commissioned by Jesus Christ Himself. As St. Paul warned: if anyone should offer a gospel or revelation different from the one given to the Apostles and the Church, it should be rejected.

Guidelines of the Church

The Church uses certain criteria and principles to discern the truth and authenticity of revelations, apparitions and supernatural phenomena. People are well advised to keep these principles in mind in discerning cases of the allegedly supernatural things.

(1) **Regarding the person or persons directly involved in the alleged supernatural phenomena, there must be nothing that would call into question the truth of the phenomena.** For example: Is the person of sound mind and have good judgment? Is there any history of the person having any psychological or mental disorder? Is the person looking for attention or trying to appear important or special? Is the person being manipulated by others? Is the person looking for monetary or other gains? Is the person bettered spiritually by the phenomena (greater faith, humility, etc.)?

(2) **The content of the alleged revelation or apparition must not contain anything contrary to the official teachings of the Church.** Anything that is clearly against the official teachings of the Church is not of divine origin. Jesus has promised to be with the Church until the end of the world, and has given her the Holy Spirit to teach and guide her in truth. However, the mere absence of conflict with Church teachings by itself is no guarantee of the truth of a given revelation.

We have a right to expect that any true revelation from God would have a beautiful resonance with official Church teachings and make them shine more brightly. For example, the revelations to Sister Catherine Laboure in Paris in 1830 and to Bernadette Soubirous in Lourdes in 1858 resonate beautifully and clearly with the Church teaching of Our Lady's Immaculate Conception. The messages in Fatima awaken us to the already existing Church teaching that we need to pray for each other and offer reparations for our sins and the sins of others.

We also have a right to expect that any true revelation from God would be in harmony with the previous revelations that have been approved.

(3) **True apparitions or revelations from God are usually accompanied by supernatural signs which can be authenticated.** Such signs could be miraculous cures, the Stigmata, the phenomena connected with ecstasies, Eucharistic miracles, etc. These signs have to be authenticated by the appropriate Church authorities after utilizing the aid of competent scien-

tific expertise. The Church wants to make sure that for these signs there is no purely natural explanation and no possibility of any diabolical intervention. It must also be ascertained that there is no fraud or trickery.

(4) The fruit that comes directly as a result of the apparition or revelation must be solid spiritual fruit worthy of God. Among such fruit we would expect: repentance for sin, conversion and amendment of life, greater love for God and neighbor, greater faith, humility, obedience to proper Church authorities, patience, resignation to God's Will, making more and better use of the Sacraments (especially Reconciliation/Confession and the Holy Eucharist) and better attendance at Mass..

By the same token, when the fruits of an apparition or revelation are such that lead people spiritually astray, it is a bad reflection on the source. For example, some bad fruits would be: pride, hating or despising others, disobedience to Church authorities, contradicting official Church teachings, disregard for the Sacraments, setting up the apparition or seers or revelation in opposition to the Church or in place of the Church, causing spiteful or jealous divisions in the Church. All such things do not speak well of the apparition, if they stem from it.

Some final points

When discerning the things of God we always need **humility**. We also need **prayer**, asking God for light to know His truth and grace to do His Will. We should not allow ourselves to be carried away by anything that is not of God. Since God has given us the guidance of His Mystical Body, the Church, we should rely on the Church for knowing the truth, and love the Church (as did Jesus Himself and all the Saints), for helping us to live the truth in holiness.

Foreword

The human race could have lost all hope when our first parents, Adam and Eve, misused their free will and disobeyed God. With His infinite Goodness and Mercy, however, God left the door to our salvation open by sending His Only Son as our Redeemer so that everyone who accepts Him and His Teachings may attain eternal life.

In order to continue His Redemptive Work until the end of the world, Christ established His Church and, through the Holy Spirit, is guiding and protecting her from the fury of hell. Christ's Church, which is one, holy, and catholic and stands on the Apostolic foundation, is God's Way of leading us to salvation by teaching us the full and infallible truth and by channeling His graces to us.

This reality of the Divine Presence, Teachings and Distribution of Graces through the Church, however, does not mean that our salvation will be automatic or even easy. We still have our free will to exercise as well as our human nature weakened by the original and personal sins and the evil influences from the world and the devil to cope with.

In fact, the devil has been intensifying his efforts to prevent us from correctly understanding God's Infinite Goodness, His True Presence among us, and His Redemption of humans at work through His Church. The numerous heresies throughout Church History and the current revolts and disorders in the Church can be understood in the context of the devil's attempts to mislead us and, thus, destroy our true faith.

God chose Our Lady, not only as the instrument by which the Incarnation of the Second Divine Person could begin two thousand years ago, but as the Helper to Our Savior throughout His Redemptive Work until the end of the world. As Eve helped Adam to disobey God in an essential way, Our Lady assists her Divine Son in saving us in an essential way. God could have chosen a different way, but He didn't. He willed that Mary, the Second Eve, participate as the Helper in Christ's redemptive activities including His terrible sufferings, and that she reveal His infinite Love and Compassion for His poor children as their true Mother. God filled her with His graces from the moment of her Conception so that she may channel them abundantly to His children and that she may effectively overcome the devil. This is exactly the reason why Our Lady has been coming to us repeatedly, especially since the 16th Century in Guadalupe, Mexico, anxiously imploring and helping us to turn away from sins, to open our eyes to the truths and the means of salvation deposited in the Holy Catholic Church and to participate in Christ's Redemptive Work for our fellow humans, following her example. Acquiring a true understanding of Mary's role for our salvation, which has been so obscured in recent years, and positively responding to Christ's Call to carry our own crosses and participate in His Redemptive Work lie at the heart of Our Lady's messages.

Following her apparitions and signs in Guadalupe (1531), Paris (1830), LaSalette (1846), Lourdes (1858), Fatima (1917), Akita (1972), and more, Our Lady's efforts to rescue her children seem to be reaching a climax through her activities in the small, insignificant-looking city of Naju, Korea. Through the messages and signs she is bringing to us in Naju, Our Lady is prodding us to rediscover the value and power of the spiritual treasures God entrusted to His Church. We are in a spiritual and moral crisis in our world and Church today, not because God's help is lacking, but because we have misused our free will through pride and complacency, neglecting what is already abundantly available to us and thus acquiring a diluted and distorted perception of God's Revelations to us. That is why Our Lady is weeping so sorrowfully, imploring us to wake up and to reform our lives before it becomes too late.

All of the messages that Julia Kim in Naju received from Our Lord and Our Lady between July 1985 and January 1996 are contained in a different book: ***Messages of Love—The Mother of the Savior Speaks to the World from Naju, Korea***, which also includes Julia's narrations explaining the circumstances surrounding the messages such as visions, sufferings, Eucharistic miracles, other signs and so on. In contrast, this book contains only a selection of the messages which are compiled according to subject, for the purpose of helping readers grasp the main points in the messages more clearly and more quickly. It is important that we read the messages with a humble, loving and prayerful mind, listening to Our Lord and Our Lady as Their beloved and yet unworthy children. That way, we can make progress in understanding the immense love and mercy flowing from the Sacred Heart of Jesus and the Immaculate Heart of Mary. It will be a waste of time, if one reads the messages out of curiosity and human calculation, seeking concrete predictions, for example. It is also necessary that we read the same messages repeatedly over time and meditate on them, because these messages are intended to induce real changes in our lives, which is possible only when they permeate deeply into our hearts. It was Our Heavenly Mother's promise *(June 29, 1987 and February 4, 1988)* that our souls would be renewed with her love and mercy, when we accept and practice her messages.

Sang M. Lee
Editor & Translator
February 11, 1996

THE MESSAGES

My Tears and Tears of Blood

Because I love you all, I am holding on to you all even to the extent of vomiting blood. . . in order to save even one more soul that is failing. (November 5, 1986)

Display the power of love. My Heart is hurting so much because of the deafness and blindness of the children who do not love. Because they do not repent and, therefore, sink deeper into sins, my Heart is burning and burning so much that it bleeds. The blood gets mixed with tears and flows out of my eyes. Even so, they do not accept my words and, because of this, the anger of God is flaming up very vehemently. (October 14, 1989)

Accept me warmly with prayers, sacrifices, reparations and the offerings of consecrated hearts and sufferings. Thus, wipe away my tears and tears of blood shed for you by letting me live in your everyday life. By doing so, you will be preparing a place where Jesus, Who will be coming in glory, can reside. (March 25, 1991)

Jesus and Mary suffer for our sins

Do you know how the Heart of my Son Jesus is being torn apart? His Heart is being torn apart continuously, as human sins multiply and disorder spreads. Make reparations. (July 15, 1985)

Do not weep for my tears, but look at and console my Son Jesus who wears a crown of thorns and sheds blood and sweat. (August 11, 1985)

Listen to the sounds of nails being driven on me. I am being crucified together with my Son. (October 22, 1986)

Nobody fully understands my sufferings. I have difficulty breathing because of the sinners. You must help me. Many priests are avoiding me. (October 19, 1987)

You must understand well what kind of sacrifice my Son Jesus made for you and through what kind of pains your salvation has been won. (October 14, 1989)

In this age, my Immaculate Heart is covered with a crown of thorns, which are so sharp and hurting. Make me known hurriedly with greater love and sacrifices. This Mother feels extreme pains in her Heart, as she looks at more and more souls who fall victim to Satan's temptations every day. (February 16, 1994)

My beloved daughter! Even in this current age, my Son Jesus is suffering on the Cross shedding much Blood and covered with Blood to save this world permeated with sins. This Mother who watches this is also bleeding from her torn Heart. (January 18, 1995)

On Abortions and Birth Control

My Heart is broken because of the unlimited birth control. Prevent abortions and pray for those who carry out abortions. (July 15, 1985)

Because of birth control and abortions, I feel extreme pains in my womb. Little lives are roaming about in limbo after having been deprived of their human dignity and treated only as a lump of bloody flesh—which was a consequence of the human cruelty, desecration and the failure to recognize the dignity of human life. Pray and soothe their wounds and offer atonements for the sins commited at night. (November 5, 1986)

Look! Many souls are going toward hell because of abortions. I have to implore with tears like this in order to save those numerous souls. I intend to save them through you—through your sacrifices and reparations. How can I be unaware of the pains you endure? Now, would you participate in the pains of the little babies who have been abandoned by their ignorant

2

and cruel parents? (May 12, 1987)

People are carrying out abortions even at this moment, causing intense pain in my womb. Pray the rosary more fervently. (January 30, 1988)

People are walking on the road toward hell, because they commit cruel murders and yet do not know that they are murderers. These little lives are deprived of their human dignity and receive terrible punishments that their parents deserve. Aren't these punishments too cruel for them? (July 29, 1988)

I am overcome with sorrow, because these innocent lives, precious lives given by God, are cruelly trampled, brutally kneaded, crushed, torn, and killed by ignorant and indifferent parents. (July 29, 1988)

Therefore, I want to show you these little babies begging for their lives and, thereby, convert many sinners and bring them back to me. Tell everyone that a little baby is not a bloody lump, but has a life flowing in it from the moment of conception in the mother's womb. (July 29, 1988)

Our Lady's Intense Love for Us

Spread the fire of love that is flaming up in my Heart. (July 15, 1985)

I love you despite your weaknesses. I want all of your love to be directed toward me. (June 29, 1987)

Forget about your weaknesses and remember my love. As my love will sustain you in your weaknesses, empty your hearts. Only then will I be able to work in you. Give me even your present sufferings. There are always some temptations to overcome in this world. (January 10, 1988)

On Family

I want you to be happy. A husband and a wife are joined together so that they may lead a happy life. But my Son becomes broken-hearted when they hate each other and do not forgive each other. You must love one another. Who are your closest neighbors? How can you say that you love me and love the Lord when you cannot even love those in your family? Sanctify your family through love and harmony. This is what my Son Jesus thirsts for. (July 15, 1985)

Look around you. This world is being covered with darkness, as sins multiply. There cannot be peace in the world, because many families are getting sick. The couples combined together to live a happy life are becoming isolated individuals, as they are unable to forgive and love each other and are becoming jealous, resentful and hateful of each other. My daughter, see how serious family troubles are.

She showed me (Julia) the scenes of many families, as in a movie.

Only a few were trying to live according to the Lord's Will. The sick families looked so terrible and miserable. Conflicts between mothers-in-law and daughters-in-law, between husbands and wives, among brothers and sisters, and between parents and children. . . Their eyes were burning with hatred and permeated with poison. They were hating each other, because their thinking was self-centered. As the adults were fighting and hurting each other, their children were being trampled on. The wounds gave rise to more wounds.

What a tragedy that they had to go on living like this! Insisting on equal rights between men and women. . . being unforgiving to each other. . . The devils were clapping their hands and giggling in an ugly manner for the divisions and hatred they had promoted. Even those who believed in God were falling into temptations frequently because of their weakness. This was offending the Lord and giving Him such sorrows. (March 13, 1987)

To the Workers of Mary

Achieve unity among those who do my work. In doing so, become sacrificial victims. Those who are working for me and for Jesus lack unity among themselves. As the Father, the Son and the Holy Spirit are One, you must become one, too. Be a good example to others by uniting in humility. (July 15, 1985)

Together with those brothers and sisters whom I united with you spiritually, pray, do penance and sacrifices and approach me walking the way of a little person with humility. My spirit is flowing in you and in them. So, work together. Also tell my beloved priests that the way of the martyrs is a narrow and difficult one and is like a sailboat in the middle of a violent storm. But tell them that I will sustain them and be with them always. (October 24, 1986)

Daughter! Many of my children testifying for me are living without self-renunciation and, therefore, are unable to spread love as they should. (June 29, 1987)

My daughter! Have a special love for my children with whom you work. The devils of pride, envy and resentment have an eye on them, because they try to become higher. You must practice love through sacrifices. Didn't I tell you that all the devils will be defeated when you practice love? Unite by loving one another. (January 10, 1988)

Different responsibilities are assigned to all of you, as you are different members of the same body and have different functions. Do not refuse the cross given to you. I will purify you by placing you in the furnace of my love and melting your impurities. Children, achieve unity. (January 30, 1988)

Daughter, look. I have chosen numerous souls with love, but they are giving much pain to my Son Jesus by considering themselves lofty and deserting my messages, which amounts to a betrayal. Jesus continues suffering on the Cross, because they scourge Him cruelly and despise and insult Him. (February 4, 1988)

In order to save the children who are wandering in a worsening darkness, I continue pouring down the light from my Immaculate Heart upon them. But even my closest children are not renouncing themselves and are hurting my Heart intensely! (August 29, 1989)

Daughter! Now many children are following me superficially by compromising with the corruptible flesh and the world permeated with errors. I am very sad, because there are only very few children who are following me truly with their hearts. (August 15, 1990)

Follow my words quickly. I cannot wait any longer. You will see the flames of my Immaculate Heart blinding Satan and performing miracles of love in union with you, who have been called, just as the Lord turned water into wine at the wedding in Cana. (November 28, 1991)

5

I called you specially, asking for your prayers and reparation for the conversion of sinners. If you unite with each other in love and follow me, you will become a large net of love. The Lord will use you as a net that catches people and, thus, will accomplish salvation. (May 31, 1992)

Stay awake all the time. The devils fear and hate you so much now. They will try furiously to topple you with all kinds of wicked schemes, but do not forget that I am always at your side guarding and protecting you. (February 16, 1994)

My beloved children! Regardless of what happens, do not stop or hesitate but go forward courageously. God has allowed free will to humans. Therefore, if people do not follow God's Will, they cannot be forced. But today I offered up my daughter who has been suffering death agonies, those priests who have been called to work for me, and other children who have responded to my call, to God on the altar of my Immaculate Heart. Therefore, remember this offering and follow me, throwing away everything and as more and more humble and little persons. Then, you will become the light that dispels darkness. (July 5, 1995)

Many do not understand the Infinite Love of God

As there are many children who do not understand the Infinite Love of God and are wandering among superficial things, I will gather children from all over the world and reveal to them the amazing miracles of love. I want my beloved daughter and you, who are her brothers and sisters, to join hands and give me devoted service in unity. (November 25, 1991)

Humilty, love and consecration are the foundation for all good works

Oh, my beloved children! Thank you. Now that you are holding my hands, you will get to Heaven with Faith, Hope and Love. Let's hurry and begin our work. The beginning is important. Once begun, there will be difficulties, too, but the Lord will protect you from the beginning to the end. Humility, love and consecration are the foundation for all good works. Begin more humbly. (November 28, 1991)

Love, respect, obey and pray for priests

Pray for priests without ceasing. They are now like a light before wind. They are being subjected to temptations. The windows of rectories are left open. Through the open windows, three devils *(of pride, materialism and lust)* are peeking in. Close the windows of rectories. (August 11, 1985)

Become sacrificial offerings for priests. I am helping them, too. So, support them to the end, because they are my most precious and beloved sons. (August 11, 1985)

Pray for priests ceaselessly. Your severe pains to the extent of shedding blood and sweat will help priests. When priests work to help those people who fell into errors because of their ingratitude, how can they be liberated from their sins, unless your sacrifices and reparations accompany (the priests' work)? (April 18, 1987)

Today I shed tears of love burning in my Immaculate Heart for my most beloved priests to wash their wounds and console their hearts. I want you to become their comforters, too. (April 23, 1987)

My most beloved priests are now walking on the path of loneliness and a painful cross. They are climbing Mt. Calvary tired and suffering. They are walking on an alienated path of the cross, suffering many pains in their wounds. Help them. For the conversion of sinners who are deeply mired in evil habits and to follow the Will of my Son Jesus, priests are carrying the burden of teaching the way of love to the numerous souls who despise and ignore them countless times and the burden of offering sacrifices and reparations for those souls. I want you to pray with me for them so that they may not be infected by the world but be faithful to their vocation. They are my sons who deserve respect and love by all. (April 23, 1987)

Listen well and tell people. From now on, all of you must treat priests and religious like your parents who gave birth to you.

You must also become their comforters. That is because this age is very evil and filled with errors and, because of this, the devils are so active and are employing all the available means to destroy priests. They know that they gain more by ruining one priest than destroying one thousand or ten thousand lay people. (April 23, 1987)

Now, look. Those who left the priesthood had been good priests. That is why I am praying, shedding tears that they do not walk on the road to hell but repent. I want you to pray for them, too. (April 23, 1987)

Now, look! Many priests are suffering because of the criticisms by those who have family-life vocations. How can you, who have been called to family life, judge priests and religious, while not being faithful to your own vocations? Why are you trying to remove the speck from others' eyes while missing the plank in your own? (April 23, 1987)

I implore you today to wash the wounds of my priests whom I love so much that I can put them in my eyes without feeling any pain. *(This is an idiomatic expression in Korea used by adults about the children whom they love very much.)* (April 23, 1987)

I want the lay people to obey the Pope, Cardinals, Bishops and all the priests. They are my most beloved sons and have received the power to forgive the sins of countless people who have become contaminated with sins. For this reason, even my Son Jesus comes down from Heaven to earth in obedience to them. (June 29, 1987)

Greater sacrifices and self-denial are necessary, because the majority of the shepherds are falling into errors, as they are not leading a life according to the Gospels. (November 6, 1988)

My Son Jesus comes to you through priests to give you His Blood. So, pray much that priests, who should be holy, may not fall into temptations, that they may become holier and worthily carry out their duty of giving His Blood to people so that they may not have anything to be ashamed of as the givers of the Blood of Jesus in His place, and that the Church, families and society may become united as one, as the Father, the Son and the Holy Spirit are One. (January 15, 1989)

All the children in the world! As John did together with me, all of you must stand at the foot of the Cross with all your love, meditating on those hours when Jesus offered sacrifices. You must help priests so that they may carry their heavy crosses well. Do not fear the world, even if it does not understand or accept you when you try to practice justice. My burning Immaculate Heart will always be your home and your refuge. (April 8, 1993)

To the Priests

I ask the Pope, Cardinals, Bishops and all priests. You must carry the cross and pray together at Gethsemane in order to save this world contaminated with errors. Share the pains that my Son's Sacred Heart and my Immaculate Heart suffer. Always be awake and pray at Gethsemane to avoid falling into sins of impurity. Love alone will lead you to Jesus. Oh, my sons! Live with me so that I may not be disappointed. Offer up small sacrifices, because my Heart is filled with sorrows for those who commit sins. (May 17, 1987)

Offer sacrifices and reparations without ceasing for the Pope, Cardinals, Bishops and priests. They, too, must accept my messages, but many don't. In order to prevent the chastisement, my beloved priests must accept the messages quickly. I wouldn't spare anything for the Pope, Cardinals, Bishops and all the priests. . . . (January 15, 1989)

Oh, my beloved priests, my sons! Today, I bestow streams of mercy on you out of my Immaculate Love. Your High Priest, my Son Jesus, also bestows the cup of blessing on you today. Thank you for fighting in the world of darkness where many souls have lost faith and are revolting against God and blaspheming Him because of their selfishness. (July 5, 1989)

My dear sons! I know well that you are experiencing many pains, fatigue, loneliness, sadness, and, sometimes, blasphemies and insults in following my Son Jesus. But that is unavoidable. Think of all the scourgings that my Son received. He was the Son of God, but, because He was Jesus with a human nature, He suffered pains when He was ridiculed and crucified. Then, for the salvation of the human race, He asked His Father to forgive those who were hurting Him. He did not drink the bitter chalice, because He wanted to, did He? He said, *"Father, if You will, remove this chalice from Me; but not My Will, but Yours be done."* (July 5, 1989)

Oh, my beloved priests! My sweet priests whom I can put in my eyes without feeling any pain. Give me all your pains and sufferings. Come to me and spread my messages of love courageously so that people may be freed from the Red Dragon and that the Kingdom of the Lord may come. In union with the Pope and all the Bishops, let the victory of the Resurrection reach the whole world. In this age, the devil is becoming more active to control humans by means of human powers. My numerous poor children are following the Red Dragon and walking toward the deep darkness, hell, in their extreme pride. They are working in many different cunning ways to confuse people about the messages that I give. (July 5, 1989)

Oh, my dear priests! I want even the most corrupt souls to receive the light from me. Therefore, be loyal to Jesus so that they may convert. Also, do not let my tears and blood flow in vain. I want my beloved priests to become sacrificial victims for the conversion of sinners. Now, the devils are influencing people in the guise of all kinds of good. Oh, my sons! Shouldn't you discern (what the devils are doing) and defeat the devils? That is what is called for in my messages. Pray the rosary fervently. Offer sacrifices and reparations and consecrate yourselves totally to the Sacred Heart of Jesus. Trust more and follow me with confidence. Let all my children offer more rosary prayers for world peace—as prayers of love and unity. (July 5, 1989)

Oh, my beloved priests! My precious ones who perform the amazing miracle of the Sacrament! Do not turn your eyes away from my messages, but have complete trust in my Immaculate Heart and entrust everything to my guidance. Rely totally on my Immaculate Heart through unending sacrifices and penances in order to crush the devils who are trying to afflict you by all kinds of cunning methods. My Immaculate Heart will surely triumph. You will certainly see the victory, if you accept my words. I will help you with my power that crushes the head of the serpent and I will be with you. But, if you do not accept my words, many people will not be able to avoid the chastisement from God. (July 5, 1989)

Now, come back to me and work together with me. Oh, the little priests of my Jesus! Sacred ministers of Jesus! Hold my hands. I ask each of you, who are my most precious and beloved little Jesus. Please put into practice the messages I give through Julia, who is so little and poor. (July 5, 1989)

I make a special request to all priests. Imitate Jesus, the Teacher, Who sacrificed all of Himself, and give all the children in the world the Love He showed to the disciples at the Last Supper. Do not look to the world, but to Jesus Who suffered the agony of death on the Cross. Then, you will become faithful priests. (April 8, 1993)

My beloved priests! Get closer together and hold each other's hands hurriedly. And achieve unity in total love. The devil will cause more confusion employing many different methods, but do not fall into his cunning schemes and stop spreading the messages. If you do not help me, I cannot do anything, either. Hurry up and bring those numerous sheep, which have been lost and are wandering, to the refuge of my Immaculate Heart. I need you, because I want to save all the children through you. (April 14, 1993)

My beloved priests! Do not forget my wish to bestow on all of you the combined love from the Sacred Heart of Jesus and my Immaculate Heart that are burning, but follow me energetically and courageously, united in complete trust and love and with the faith that has been entrusted to you. (May 27, 1993)

All the priests in the world! How corrupt and polluted this world is! Promotion of dissensions through intrigues and contradictions, sacrilegious activities, irresponsible behaviors, slanders because of jealousy, greed—the desire to possess all instead of sharing with others, corruption through avarice, and the attempt to justify all kinds of moral disorders through pride—all these are the cunning enemies that make souls decay. (May 27, 1993)

My beloved priests! When you spread my messages of love which I give you shedding tears and tears of love, you will experience pains, too. But I will elevate you, who have been called from all over the world, to a high level of sanctity so that you may reveal the true identity of the errors and promote the Truth with your mouths which will be like two-edged swords and thus may spread the fragrance of Christ. All the falsehood, plots, tricks and cunning slanders will disappear in the presence of the light from God the Father, just as fog clears under the sun. (November 24, 1994)

GOD THE FATHER: If priests, who are ministers of Jesus and were chosen by Me through My Son, do not listen to My Words and continue to judge and criticize them, the sheep which are following them will also continue to walk toward hell. They must keep in mind that My Judgment will be fierce. They are blocking the Gate of Heaven with their knowledge, leaving numerous souls to loiter and wander outside. I cannot tolerate this any longer. When one priest is ruined, it is not just he who is ruined. Many souls fall together with him. This gives Me extreme sorrows. (June 16, 1995)

My beloved priests! You were given the power to change bread and wine into the Body, Blood, Soul and Divinity of the Lord in the Church. You were also given the power to forgive sins. Therefore, hurriedly teach the Mystery of the Eucharist to all so that they may make sincere Confessions and receive the Eucharist with clean hearts. Help them follow the Lord. (July 2, 1995)

I ask my beloved priests to help all those who thirst and crave for worldly things to truly repent and return to the Lord through the Eucharistic Signs that have been given through the little soul who professes to be unworthy and unqualified. All these should be for God's glory and for the salvation of souls. Entrust all the rest to me. When you follow me entrusting everything to me, your union with God through His Incarnation will continue in the Mystery of the Eucharist. This union is unprecedented and beyond human description. (July 2, 1995)

You can go to Jesus through the cross

The path that leads to my Son Jesus is a narrow and difficult one of the cross. The human race can be saved by this path, but most do not come near it. (September 15, 1985)

My beloved daughter! Do not feel so sad. Am I not with you? Do you think the path that the Saints and martyrs walked was an easy one? It was a narrow and dangerous path of the cross. Now, hold my hands and those of your brothers and sisters. Let's go together to the flower garden of paradise, where the martyrs and Saints are. (October 24, 1986)

When you come to me by walking on the path of a little and poor person, which is a narrow and difficult path, a painful and lonesome path, and a dangerous, thorny path, I will hold your hands. So, come to me. You will receive heavenly consolations. Come to me by becoming a lowlier and lowlier person. I am preparing a laurel crown for you. (February 25, 1987)

Nothing can be achieved without sacrifices. The road to Heaven is difficult. But know that there are joyful relaxing places there. (November 26, 1989)

All the children in the world! I ask all the souls not to listen to the sounds of evil. The devils rejoice so much when they take joy away from you. They cause division among people and press down their hearts with darkness and sorrows. So, be watchful all the time and carry your cross well, even when it feels too heavy. If you lay down the cross thinking that it is too heavy, evil, which has been waiting for that moment, may enter you right away. I implore you ardently. (January 18, 1995)

The Need for Unity

As the Father, the Son and the Holy Spirit are One, you must all become one, too, and console me. (October 19, 1986)

I will dwell in you, if you renounce yourselves and come to me. Unite with one another in love. If you do, Satan will retreat. Become apostles of my Immaculate Heart. Console me by doing so. (November 5, 1986)

Achieve unity by loving one another. I want you to trust each other, be respectful and faithful to each other, and fulfill your duties. (February 13, 1987)

If you do not unite, more blood will flow from my eyes and I will suffer more. Give alms to me. Give alms to this Heavenly Beggar. (January 30, 1988)

As God is Three Persons in One, I am the one Mother of Heaven for all of you. As the Father, the Son and the Holy Spirit are One, you must also all become one. (June 30, 1990)

The Need for Penance

This world is decaying with sins. Even with the Sacred Blood of my Son Jesus, it is difficult to appease the just anger of God the Father. Let me borrow your body and your mouth. (October 20, 1986)

I have implored with tears at many places in the world. It has been very difficult to find souls who are consecrated to converting sinners by participating in sufferings with me for the sake of my Son Jesus and me (October 21, 1986)

Therefore, my sons and daughters, become persons smashed and trampled by all the people of this world and offer even these matters as penance. Then, you will come to me as humble persons, as little persons. . . . (February 13, 1987)

Even at this moment, it is necessary to make more sacrifices and do penance because of the sins being committed by many of my children. For this reason, you need to suffer more. By doing this, you are participating in my sufferings. (June 29, 1987)

I am carrying the burden of reparation for you; so carry the burden for others. There are too many souls who fall into hell and bruise my Heart. When you offer penance and prayers to compensate for the sins and ingratitude of so many souls, they will be saved. (June 29, 1987)

In order to save many souls, we must carry the cross of love together and offer reparations with prayers and sacrifices and, thereby, appease the just anger of God the Father. (October 19, 1987)

You understand that there can be birth because of the pains of labor that you suffer now, don't you? Help save many souls by patiently suffering these pains and remember the rewards that I am preparing for you. (January 10, 1988)

My daughter! My Son Jesus paid a dear price to save the poor, sinful souls—the souls who are walking toward ruin because of their hypocrisy, ingratitude and indifference. Do not have any doubt in following my wish that you offer your sufferings gracefully to lead many souls to the path of salvation. Also, believe that when you suffer much, you accumulate much joy in Heaven. (February 4, 1988)

Deeply sorrowful lamentations, silent prayers, and crying out to Heaven because of betrayals, ingratitude and enormously heavy pressures; the pains of death experienced by my Divine Son for the salvation of the whole human race. . . Your participation in these pains will bring about the conversion of many sinners. Therefore, do not be troubled, but carry the cross further. (November 26, 1989)

My daughter who follows me suffering pains! Even today, I am calling, through your sufferings, my little and weak souls who will fight a difficult fight against the evil force that causes afflictions and temptations day and night. Offer your sufferings more gracefully. I intend to collect the seeds of martyrdom from the sufferings of my little souls, plant them in the Garden of my Immaculate Heart, so that flowers will blossom from these seeds of goodness. Therefore, prepare many good seeds. They will be used in saving many humans and countries at the decisive time of tribulation. (August 15, 1990)

The souls who are elevated high on the Cross and offer themselves gracefully as victims to the Lord are truly the souls who glorify the Lord and are the little souls who are closest to me. I want all the children to become completely humble and to be tightly embraced in my bosom of love like the Baby Jesus. I will make you spread the strong fragrance of my Motherhood to all the corners of the world. (September 17, 1991)

Numerous sins are being committed with eyes

I cannot look at those numerous sins committed with eyes. You and I are doing penance for these sins. You are also suffering the pains for the aborted babies and for the conversion of those poor souls who carry out abortions. These pains will not be in vain. (July 27, 1988)

Our Lady's statue in Naju represents the Mother of Mercy, the same as on the Miraculous Medal. She promises protection and care to everyone who seeks her help.

Jesus: Admit your sins in a simple and humble way

Jesus: Admitting your sins in a simple and humble way and in obedience, aspire ever more strongly for the little person's way of Love, loving and trusting My Mother. Then, your attachment to pleasures, reputation, social status, power, material goods, pride and face-saving will be replaced by heroic deeds. (December 8, 1992)

Abandon your ego and walk the way of a little person's love

Renounce your ego and abandon selfishness. I will be your shield. Even the arrows of fire thrown by the devils will not harm you. Pray much without worrying. I want you to stand on my side and become courageous guides in saving this world permeated with evil. (October 20, 1986)

When you do renounce yourselves and come to me, I will become your strength. I will give energy to the weak souls and help them free themselves from sins. (April 21, 1987)

You will live in my Immaculate Heart. So, rejoice and keep your hearts on heavenly matters, desire heavenly things, renounce self-love and walk the way of self-renunciation and of a little person's love. Come back to my bosom and become a comfort to me. (January 30, 1988)

I am imploring you again and again, because I want to save you all from this dangerous world. Therefore, renounce your ego and follow my wishes well. Then, darkness will retreat from this world, and the Kingdom of the Lord will come. (April 21, 1991)

When you renounce your ego and follow me completely by practicing my messages of love and by making my Immaculate Heart that is burning with love known to all the children in the world, you will experience pains. But your souls will be purified and made stronger, as gold becomes purified in fire. If you follow me in unity, what you have lost in the world will turn into eternal joy by gaining me. (May 23, 1991)

Become children. Know clearly that Satan leads you to judge with your own ideas and behave as adults, feeling self-confident, and, thus, makes you fall into a trap. You must gain Heaven by offering yourselves up with a child's heart. (February 18, 1993)

If a grain of wheat falls to the ground and dies, it produces much fruit. But if it does not die, it remains just a grain of wheat. Salvation came to this world, only because there was the painful Sacrifice of Calvary by my Son Jesus. Repent hurriedly and become a floral crown of joy for Him. (April 8, 1993)

In this time of purification, numerous children on vast continents join hands with the devil, think and speak with an adult's mind, mobilize all the human knowledge and wisdom and, as a result, make wrong judgments and behave accordingly. Because of this, they loiter around outside the Sacred Heart of Jesus and my Immaculate Heart and do not understand the words of their Heavenly Mother. This gives me much pain in my Heart. (September 24, 1994)

The Status of the Current World

The sins in the world are so numerous that God the Father's just anger has reached an extremely high level (October 21, 1986)

Even within countries, people are fighting in division rather than uniting and are trampling peace by hating instead of loving each other. Thus, the fire in my Immaculate Heart is flaming up intensely, because people are not practicing my messages, become fanatic slaves of the world, close their hearts to the precious opportunities to share love and are wasting everything because of their selfishness. . . . This is a time when nations are confronting each other, causing evil to spread in all directions and making the dangers more imminent. I ask for more prayers with trust and love so that nations may unite with each other, individuals may join together and, thus, the Kingdom of the Sacred Heart may be established. (November 6, 1988)

Do you know about the Deluge in the time of Noah and the Tower of Babel? Who can say that the sins now are less than in those times? (January 8, 1989)

Because love has been destroyed, there is no unity among people. As a result, the outcries of human beings in the midst of their sins are turning into noises of wars, which, in turn, are reaching Heaven and provoking God's anger. (January 29, 1989)

Daughter! Look at the condition of many children in this world. Because people complain even about small pains like headaches, bruises and scratches, the devils are laying traps of thorns, venom and atrocities. The human feet should be used for rushing to adore God, but are, instead, being used for running toward evil things. Their mouths should be used for praising and admiring the Son of God, but are being used for blaspheming and judging God. As a result, the whole world is being covered with darkness and is provoking the anger of God. The punishment is imminent. (October 14, 1989)

In this age, the devils corrupt numerous peoples' consciences, making them commit sins of impurity, even leading to murders; destroy human dignity by abortions; drag them into errors and all kinds of sins such as corruption, injustice, curses, violent words, hatred and revenge; and make them walk the way of selfishness. How sorrowful my Son Jesus feels when He sees all these children! (November 11, 1990)

This world is decaying with corruption and degradation. The human race is facing a crisis under black clouds, and sins are spreading like a horrible cancer. The storm is already becoming violent. This world is exposed to a grave danger, as the storm rages on. How would this Heavenly Mother feel in her Heart, as she watches all this? (January 29, 1991)

You must also remember that, as birth comes nearer, pains will intensify. Because governments, peoples and societies are resisting the God of Justice, they become surrounded by a huge darkness. Because they are not opening their doors widely to Christ Who is coming, various tribulations and agonies are resulting. (March 25, 1991)

Daughter! Make haste. Should the cup of God's wrath overflow onto this dark world which is like a desert? Events are unreeling already, but there are too few priests who are following me. The whole world is filled with dangers and is going through pains of labor. There are countless souls who need spiritual and physical help. Right now, God's work of salvation stands on nothingness and worthlessness. I want to gather all the children, who are struggling with weakness, poverty and fierce battles with evil, into my burning Immaculate Heart. (May 8, 1991)

There has never been another time when the world was so filled with Satan's temptations and with sins, and afflicted so much pain on the Lord's Heart as now. Look! Even at this moment, people are dying because of droughts, earthquakes and volcanic eruptions. In so many other ways, numerous people are dying. (February 6, 1993)

Daughter! More and more children are falling into the sweet temptations by the devil, who has tried to compete against God with a preposterously big ambition. They do not realize in what kind of a situation they are and receive Communion sacrilegiously. They are earning more and more of God the Father's just anger . . . My beloved daughter! In this manner, they get lost and are wandering in darkness. They cannot even recognize themselves. How can they understand themselves, when they have lost even the sense of direction? First, they walk in a fog, then, in darkness, and, then, far away from the source of love, totally forgetful of the Lord's Divine Nature and blind and deaf spiritually. Where would they be going? This Heavenly Mother desires to save all the children who have been lost, with your help. (July 2, 1995)

Live a consecrated life

It is time to consecrate yourselves to me. Why do you hesitate again and again? I am asking you for this together with my Son Jesus because of the pains in Our Hearts caused by many who do not live a consecrated life. (October 23, 1986)

Live a consecrated life filled with constant prayers, sacrifices, penance and love. (March 13, 1987)

Every day, lower yourself further, thinking about Jesus on Mt. Calvary. Through poverty, humility, obedience and purity, keep going down from the high place to the low place following this Mother who wants you to walk the way of perfection. Shouldn't we become more humble like Jesus, Who chose to be humble? Change your life further—throwing away every attachment. Change your value system. Live a life of conversion. Convert every moment and converse with Jesus. Conversion does not just mean repenting sins. It means trying to live the life that God wants you to live. Abandon the worldly life and live a life based on the Gospels. Live like a lily. As the higher-grade protein gives rise to a more foul odor, the shiny things of the world entail a greater darkness. Let's die again and imitate Christ. (June 14, 1987)

Offer up everything, as I love within you, turning everything you do into a prayer of love. As you do not refuse anything to me, I will not refuse anything to you. (February 23, 1989)

The Rosary defeats the devil

Also consecrate the Blue Army. Offer more rosaries and sacrifices for world peace and human salvation. (October 23, 1986)

As I told you before, the rosary defeats the devils. Tell all the faithful to offer more decades of rosary prayers. If they pray more for the unity of this country, it will be saved from a calamity. (January 1, 1988)

Practice obedience

Practice obedience. Obey all—your superiors as well as those who are of a lower status than you. As I obeyed all, you should do the same. I feel so anxious, but will give you energy. So, do not cry but stand up courageously. What can we do, if people refuse to accept our love? Even God cannot force them. Do not expect too much too soon. Be patient and wait for the good time. (October 29, 1986)

Obedience is the precious key that opens the gate of Heaven widely. (June 21, 1995)

The Holy Eucharist

Emphasize to everyone the importance of the Holy Eucharist. By the Holy Eucharist, the Lord will be in you. He will live in you and stay there always, if you open your heart and receive

Him with a clean heart. How can the Lord enter you, if you do not have a clean heart or keep the door closed? Look at those receiving Holy Communion. . . . (October 31, 1986)

Jesus: It is My Love that prompted Me to come down to this world and call sinners rather than the just. I want everyone, without a single exception, to belong to Me, and I am relying on My Mother Mary for that. Therefore, by following her, you will be following Me. (June 5, 1988)

Jesus: Come now, all the children of the world! Today, as always, I become a sacrificial victim and am waiting for you. Let's gather at the heavenly table and share Love. When you open your heart widely and return to Me, I will not question your past, but will bestow the cup of blessing on you. (June 5, 1988)

Jesus: I am still bleeding on the Cross to save the whole human race and My Blood will not flow in vain. I am the Transfuser Who washes away your dirty sins. My Precious Blood is a special medicine that will open the eyes of the sick souls and wake up the sleeping souls—through priests. I am so troubled that people receive Me out of habit and with indifference. (June 5, 1988)

Daughter! You cannot win the victory without going through the cross. You must understand the amazing mystery of the Holy Eucharist by which God comes down from Heaven through priests in order to be with you. Therefore, make frequent Confessions to receive the Lord more worthily; open your heart widely, keep it clean and organized, and love one another so that it will become a palace and a tabernacle where the Lord can dwell. Then, the Lord will live in you, who are unworthy, and set a fire in you. (April 21, 1991)

Jesus: Daughter! Teach the Mystery of the Holy Eucharist fervently to the children who do not understand it so that the numerous people living in ingratitude may be saved through your bloody sacrifices combined with My Love. However hard I may try to give Love to them, I cannot force them to accept it, as I gave them free will. I, Who am present in the Mystery of the Holy Eucharist, am a spring that never dries, a medicine that can save the sick souls, and a doctor to the patient. (May 16, 1991)

At the Blessed Mother's request, Julia is holding hands with the Apostolic Pro Nuncio (right) and Father Raymond Spies, Julia's spiritual director (left). Moments later, the Eucharist miraculously came down and landed on Julia's tongue almost vertically. (November 24, 1994)

The Apostolic Pro Nuncio is holding the Sacred Host that miraculously came down to Julia. Father Spies and Julio Kim (Julia's husband) witness this seventh Eucharistic Miracle. (November 24, 1994)

Jesus: Daughter! Offer up more reparations for the insults by sinners. The world keeps offending, despising, insulting, scourging and bruising Me, but the burning Love of My Sacred Heart bestows the grace of mercy, forgiveness and reconciliation on so many souls who provoke the just anger of God, through the Precious Blood from the Five Wounds opened on the Cross in order to save this sick and dark world from eternal death and to give sinners eternal life. Because I love you so much, I manifest that Love by coming to you in the form of bread, hiding My Divinity, dignity and even human appearance. I come to you in person in the form of bread because of My great Love for you. But many souls pay little attention to My Real Presence, insult Me with sacrilegious Communions, and neglect Me with ingratitude. (May 16, 1991)

The Lord saved you through His Passion and Death on the Cross. He saved all of you with His Precious Blood, Wounds, and painful Death and is leading you to the Life of Resurrection through His Body and Blood in the Blessed Sacrament. Now all priests must teach the importance of the Holy Eucharist to all the children in the world, as they celebrate the Sacred Mass with true love and sincere participation. Thus, today I make this request to my beloved son, the Pope. (June 27, 1993)

How ardently has the Lord desired to share this Mystery of the Passover with you! My Son Jesus, Who shed His Precious Blood through the Five Wounds on the Cross for the salvation of His children in the world, is still coming to you as the Transfuser through the Blessed Sacrament, administered by priests, and will stay with you and live among you always. As I told you before, keep your hearts open widely all the time and make frequent Confessions so that you may receive the Lord with a clean heart. Meditate deeply on the Mystery of the Holy Eucharist and stay awake. Then, instead of the terrifying chastisement of blood and fire which is to fall upon this world, the Lord's infinite mercy and blessings of salvation will be bestowed upon you. (September 24, 1994)

Jesus: I wish to work miracles of love for all My children through the Eucharist because of My boundless Love for them, but they do not prepare themselves for receiving Me, do not realize My True Presence, insult Me with sacriligeous Communions, and, thus, neglect and betray Me. Because of this, I am deserted by numerous children and left alone in the tabernacles, waiting anxiously for them to return to Me and give love to Me. (November 2, 1994)

I have said repeatedly that the Mystery of the Holy Eucharist, which is the Bread of Life from Heaven, is a spring that never dries and a medicine that gives you salvation. But only very few are making preparations before receiving Him. If my numerous children only knew that the Eucharist is truly the Life, the Everlasting Spring, the Manna and a continuing miracle that is no less than the miracles of the Creation of the Universe and of the Redemption, they would not be walking toward hell. . . . (November 24, 1994)

The Holy Eucharist is the center of all the supernatural events, but is being trampled upon by so many children through sacrilege, insult and humiliation. Therefore, my messages of love must be spread all over the world more vigorously so that the time of the Lord, Who is present in the Eucharist, and of the New Pentecost may be advanced. (November 24, 1994)

Jesus: My real, personal and physical Presence in the Mystery of the Eucharist is an indisputable fact. I have repeatedly shown the Eucharist turning into visible Blood and Flesh so that all may believe that the Eucharist, which is a Mystery of the Infinite Love, Humility, Power and Wisdom, is My Living Presence. If certain priests do not believe in this Personal Presence of Mine in the Church, they certainly do not qualify as co-redeemers. When they ignore Me, Who is Christ, true God and true Man, they are publicly denying My Divinity while acknowledging My human nature. That is because they have lost the ability to discern between good and evil and between authentic and unauthentic. (July 1, 1995)

The Lord gave up all of Himself for your sake. He not only shed Blood two thousand years ago, but even now is squeezing all of Himself on the Cross for you, is coming to you in the form of bread and is consumed by you. If people knew this, they would not have joined forces with the devil. This great power (to change bread and wine into Jesus) in the Blessed Sacrament, a Mystery of Salvation, was not given even to Cherubim and Seraphim but was given to priests. How many

On July 1, 1995, seven Sacred Hosts descended to the altar before Our Lady's statue in the Chapel in Naju. In obedience to Archbishop Yoon's instruction, they were consumed by seven people. The Eucharist Julia received turned into visible flesh and blood in her mouth.

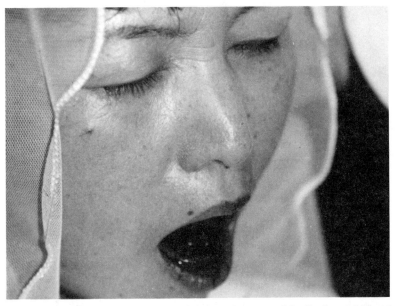

The Sacred Host in Julia's mouth turned into visible flesh and blood during Mass celebrated by Bishop Roman Danylak and two other priests on the mountain near Naju. (September 22, 1995)

of them are truly paying attention and are coming to me? (July 2, 1995)

Jesus: If my priests, who celebrate Mass every day, truly believe and feel My Real Presence and live the sublime and amazing Divine Reality, numerous souls will be purified and live in the grace from My merciful Heart beyond expectations through this Real Presence of Mine. Make My Physical Presence known hurriedly. (September 22, 1995)

Jesus: My beloved children! Do not reject My pleas which I make in this manner while being truly present in the Eucharist. If people do not want to acquire true understanding, do not follow My Will to bestow Love upon them, deny My Divinity and deny the Divine Origin (of God's revelations), then, they will face God the Father's anger. (September 22, 1995)

My Son Jesus is in Heaven, but is also present on earth with His Body, His Blood, His Soul and His Divinity, while hiding His Dignity, Humanity, and Divinity. Jesus in the Holy Eucharist will lead you to the pinnacle of prayer. (January 6, 1996)

So many children are mired in the secular spirit

So many children in the world are mired in the secular spirit. They continue committing sins, driving more nails on the Lord, pressing down the crown of thorns harder on His Head, and, thus, making Him shed more Blood. However, the Lord does not bleed in vain, but drops His Blood into a chalice and gives It to all His children through the priests whom He has called. But how many of them are accepting Him? (June 27, 1993)

Jesus: I love even the most sordid and distorted sinners

Jesus: I love even those souls who have become so sordid and distorted because of sins, because I am Love Itself. So, when they come to Me through the Sacrament of Confession, I will wash away their sins that made their souls dirty and allow them to stay in My Love. (May 16, 1991)

Entrust everything to me and rely on me

Do not worry. I know what is in your mind. Entrust everything to me and rely on me. (February 13, 1987)

Do not tremble. Have faith in the power of my Motherhood and wake up the sleeping souls. I will welcome all the repenting souls. (June 27, 1987)

I wish to be your refuge in this dangerous world. I will burn you with the flames in my Immaculate Heart. Oh, my beloved children! I will fight on your side, when you renounce yourselves and return to me. I will help you with my power that crushes the serpent. (June 30, 1987)

All of you must know well that the refuge in my bosom is always ready for the souls who have been lost, but are turning themselves to me. (November 26, 1989)

Oh, all the children of the world! It is not too late yet. Come to me in a hurry. Come to me without delay and suck the spiritual milk from my breast that is flowing out like a spring. I will make a flower garden where you can grow beautiful souls. I have left my Heart wide open to accept your pleas and requests. (October 4, 1990)

When you return to me renouncing yourselves, you will find the happiness that you have been longing for, but have not been able to find, in the bosom of this Mother of Peace, who can embrace all of you. Come to me, all of you, and let me not shed tears and tears of blood in vain. Be a comfort to my wounded Heart. By doing so, sinners will recognize my voice of love and seek the justice of God by repenting their sins in my bosom. However corrupt the souls may be, they will be forgiven with powerful flames of love when they repent. But those who sin against the Holy Spirit will not be able to avoid the fires of justice at the time of judgment. (October 4, 1990)

Let even those who are in despair, depressed, full of wounds and in tribulations suffering under the heavy pressures from their arid hearts, sins, hatred, violence and impure habits come aboard the Ark of Salvation of my Love. I will wrap them with my warm mantle and help them even in the midst of a bitterly cold snowstorm. (November 4, 1991)

My beloved children! Now offer even those trivial things in your life to me gracefully. I will give you the power to transcend even the most trivial things. When you offer up everything and drink the painful cups of the cross and martyrdom with love, even those who are deserted in the middle of the pains of death will repent and see the light in darkness. (November 4, 1991)

Walk on the path that the Saints walked

My beloved little souls! Offer yourselves up completely with your faithfulness toward me for the sake of your brethren who are severely insulting and resisting my love and also for the sake of the priests and religious who are going through the pains of labor. You must walk straight forward on the path that the Saints walked, entrusting themselves completely to me with love. There has never been a Saint who has not followed me closely. You were chosen by me for an important mission. Do not have any doubt about my protection and my love. Trust and rely on me and, thus, turn the cup of divine wrath into a cup of blessing with the intense flames of love burning in my Immaculate Heart. (August 15, 1990)

Become the apostles of My Immaculate Heart

Receive the light from my Immaculate Heart. Thus, become apostles of my Immaculate Heart who shine the light upon all the sick souls (February 13, 1987)

Do not seek your own satisfaction, but love me in a simple way. Satan's violence is increasing day after day with a terrible force. He is becoming more active to make even fervent souls reject me. Help me. I will give you the light from my Immaculate Heart so that all of you may be saved. Become apostles of my Immaculate Heart by receiving the light from my burning Heart. (May 17, 1987)

Because I called you to be the apostles of my Immaculate Heart, the devils will become more active and tempt you. Hold my hand tightly so that you may not fall into temptations. (January 30, 1988)

Participate in the Lord's Work of Salvation

My children who have faith and try to live according to the Lord's Will are going to suffer more pains. Offer up all your pains. Offer more sacrifices. If you offer sacrifices and penance out of true love, you will be helping much in saving many souls. Let everyone know this. (June 13, 1987)

Follow my will wholeheartedly to save many souls who are going toward hell without even knowing that they are going there. (November 27, 1989)

There are as many children in the world as stars in the sky and grains of sand on the beach, but only very few follow me. My beloved children! I called you today for a special purpose. As Satan's violence is increasing rapidly, I called you to participate in the Lord's work of salvation in order to save all. Participate in it by helping each other. (November 25, 1991)

In this age, I am going through the hours of death on the Cross in Gethsemane and Calvary together with Jesus again. My little soul! You are participating in the Lord's Passion together with me. So, have no fear and be strong. And have courage. (February 4, 1994)

There have already been numerous warnings, but (my children are not responding). Therefore, daughter! You need to offer up your bloody sufferings for the sake of the children in the world, meditating on the Mystery of the Passion of my Son, Jesus Christ. You have already been invited to Calvary; so, meditate on the life of Job and unite your tears, sighs, sweat and every drop of blood with the Lord's sufferings and mine and offer them up so that they may not be in vain. (February 4, 1994)

My burning Immaculate Heart is being pressed down hard by extreme pains caused by the people in the world who have betrayed God and are being controlled by the wicked devil. Daughter! You are taking part in saving this world through your severe sufferings. Therefore, offer them up well. Leave all your worries and concerns to me, your Heavenly Mother. Then, I will become the mark that indicates my working within you together with Jesus. (February 4, 1994)

Practice humility

Do not brag about anything. Instead, have humility and love. Do not own luxuries. Let's live like a pilgrim and a traveler—until you reach the bosom of your Heavenly Mother. Always be poor and little. Serve all in everything all the time. While following the footsteps of the Saints for the sake of Jesus, do not concern yourself too much with criticisms. Even when you suffer pains from others, give them peace. Through sacrifices and penance, do the things that can benefit them. (June 14, 1987)

Do not worry too much about awkward mistakes in your daily life. Do not get upset or try to defend yourself, but have trust in me. This will make you more humble. I will rescue sinners as much as you request with your sacrifices and penances. When you suffer in even small matters and begin feeling as I do, I feel comforted. (July 15, 1987)

Practice humility. This will give me a special, precious joy. Never try to become higher than others. Your penance, kindness, sacrifices, and reparations become fragrant oil for my wounds. (January 10, 1988)

Everyone has shortcomings and imperfections. But when you try to overcome them and, if you fail again, promptly repent, ask for the Lord's forgiveness and, renew the sincere resolution to amend your life, my Son Jesus and I will rejoice and help. (January 15, 1989)

I give my messages of love to the simple and little ones. Little ones give admiration, honor and glory to the Lord and do not take away anything from me. Certain things that can be shortcomings to the big souls are not shortcomings to the little ones. You are a little soul. You have many shortcomings, but these shortcomings can turn into good through sacrifices and reparations and can keep you humble. (February 23, 1989)

The gate to Heaven is small and, therefore, little children enter it. For this reason, little souls must unite with each other more solidly and follow me in order to save the world. (November 26, 1989)

As water flows to lower and lower places, my Son Jesus went down to lower places again and again. All of you must imitate my Son Jesus and become lower and lower. The bodily matters belong to the world, while the spiritual matters belong to Heaven. Following this Mother's wish that you pursue the heavenly matters only, offer up your sufferings totally and gracefully. (January 18, 1995)

Make frequent and sincere Confessions

The devils do not lead people to commit mortal sins at first. They make people commit venial sins and, then, when many venial sins have accumulated, mortal sins. Therefore, try to receive Jesus with a clean soul by making frequent Confessions, even when you only have venial sins. (June 15, 1987)

Jesus established the Sacrament of the Holy Eucharist to nurture us with His Body and Blood, to unite with us, and to resurrect our bodies after death. We must praise this amazing Sacrament, but many souls are becoming unclean by failing to make frequent Confessions. (June 15, 1987)

As you would put on freshly washed clothes before meeting a high-ranking person, prepare to receive Our Lord with a clean soul by making frequent Confessions. However hard one may try to keep the soul clean, it cannot remain spotless indefinitely. (June 15, 1987)

The Blessed Mother wept because of sacrilegious Communions. (June 15, 1987)

Jesus: My Mother Mary has often encouraged frequent Confessions. But many children make the Confession without a sincere repentance or even try to receive Me without going to Confession *(when it is necessary)*. A Confession out of habit or without true repentance is an insult to Me and will not enable one to see Me. Therefore, let Me work within you by confessing your sins with sincere repentance. (June 5, 1988)

Jesus: I also want to tell you that I desire to pour down all My Love upon all the children in this world, but too many of them cannot meet Me because they do not go to Confession. (June 5, 1988)

Practice love

Your love must be fervent. It can burn in shining flames only through unending sacrifices. (June 27, 1987)

You should know that everything will be purified through love, as gold becomes purified in the furnace. (January 10, 1988)

If you truly love me and love your neighbors, then, you are loving Jesus and will be appeasing the just anger of God the Father. When my messages are spread to the world and put into practice, the just anger of God the Father will be softened and the terrible punishment will be turned away. (January 30, 1988)

You must meet your neighbors as you would meet Jesus—with true love and a praying heart. Tell everyone. I give my love to all my children. But my Heart is hurting so much, because too many of them reject and insult my love. My ears are hurting very much because of the evil words that are so hard to listen to. (January 8, 1989)

Love leads us to victory. Strive for it with all your heart. Then, the precious grace will be allowed for the salvation of many souls. Because the sins of the world are excessive, the love of my Immaculate Heart alone is not sufficient and that is why I am calling you. (June 30, 1990)

In this age of aridity—an age of an endless desert, the victory can be won only through love. When you love, you must also shed some tears. Tears will help the seeds to bear good fruit and also help the absorption of heavenly nutrition by the souls who are hungry and have been deprived of vitality because of delinquency. (September 17, 1991)

My beloved daughter! Thank you for your loving heart and offerings. I bless all of you. I want you all to stay in my peace and become instruments of peace among all your neighbors. (January 23, 1993)

My children! You should not refuse this Mother's request that you reconcile with each other so that violence and fear may cease. (June 30, 1995)

Accept me and practice my messages of love

All the children of the world! Become even lowlier souls and follow me with confidence. As the difficulties intensify, I will stay closer to my little souls and become their strength. When all the children accept me well and put the messages of love into practice, the darkness of disorder will be defeated through the light of God's great mercy. I hope my urgent pleas will reach all the corners of the world through you. (March 25, 1991)

Jesus: If you live according to the Father's Will, live a life based on the Gospels, and put My Mother Mary's messages of love into practice, My beloved Vicar, the Pope, chosen from the whole world, will be safe and peace will come to the world. Listen to My Words and keep them in your hearts. If you refuse to live a life based on the Gospels and reject the messages of love that My Mother gives you so anxiously imploring with tears of blood, this desert-like world will experience a crisis. (January 26, 1993)

Jesus: It is not too late yet. Come to My Bosom of Love in a hurry. Didn't My Mother Mary also remind you that if you repent hurriedly and come back to me saying *"Yes,"* I will not question your past, but will embrace you in My Sacred Heart burning with Love and will bless you in the Name of the Father, the Son and the Holy Spirit? (January 26, 1993)

My beloved children! Believe like a child my words that I give you through my little soul who thinks that she is the poorest and least qualified in the world. I give these words to all of you. (February 6, 1993)

All my beloved children in the world! My messages of love will be the brake that suppresses disorder. All the children in the world must hurriedly understand my messages of love and

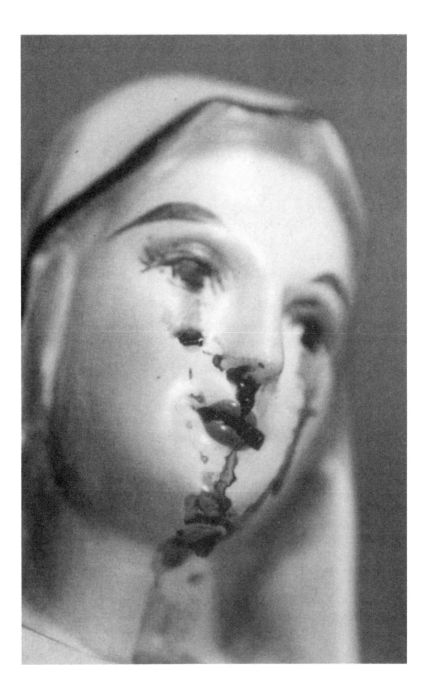

accept them. If the children in the world do not follow the Will of God and do not accept my words, God will respond with severity, and they will not be able to escape from the fire of justice. A safe tomorrow cannot be promised. (February 2, 1995)

But if you comply with the wish of this Mother who wants to carry out through you the Plan of Love and Salvation that God of the Most Holy Trinity has entrusted to me and answer with an *"Amen,"* the blazing flames of the Holy Spirit will renew this world and make it shine and you will be saved in that light. (February 2, 1995)

Children! My beloved children! Realize that the Love of my Son Jesus and me, your Heavenly Mother, is penetrating your souls, hearts and beings and rely (on Us) completely with faith and trust. Your bloody sacrifices, reparations, and prayers of love are necessary for the victory of My Son Jesus and my Immaculate Heart. Therefore, pray and follow my wishes hurriedly. Even if darkness worsens and sins spread everywhere, my burning Immaculate Heart will radiate light more brightly and you will be saved through graces and earn Heaven, if you practice my messages of love. (January 6, 1996)

My messages will change your souls

When you accept my words, my messages will renew and change your souls. In this age filled with errors, even my beloved children are being deeply permeated with errors. Because of this, I wish to spread my voice through you. I wish to save the people in the world from darkness by shining the light from my burning Immaculate Heart upon them. Therefore, become a sacrificial victim. (June 29, 1987)

Do not worry about those who are against (us). Those who have ears will hear, those who have eyes will see, and those who practice my messages are accepting me and, therefore, will experience a renewal of their souls. They will surely see the triumph of my Immaculate Heart. (January 30, 1988)

As my messages are founded on love, mercy will overflow into any soul who repents and practices the messages. (February 4, 1988)

The children who are called to the state of God's grace will experience many sufferings and temptations. But those who live according to my messages will be rewarded with a victory crown of flowers in the next world. (January 15, 1989)

My messages have been ignored

Many sheep are walking toward hell. I have implored at many places in the world with apparitions and with tears, but my messages have not been spreading well. (October 19, 1987)

My beloved daughter! I feel sorry that I always give you pains, but this Mother is suffering greater pains because of the extreme insults. Now it is an age of sins and disorder. This world is overflowing with disorder and, as a result, a great calamity is looming over the entire human race. Even if I try to hold it off, what use will it be, if the world does not repent? There has never been another age when so many children strayed so far away from repentance and brought ruin upon themselves in cooperation with the devils and under the control of the devils as now. All of them must listen to my voice of love. But, instead of listening to my earnest voice burning with love, they revolt against me with insults, criticisms and judgments, causing great damage to their souls. Because of this, my beloved little souls are suffering pains. (August 15, 1990)

Daughter! Pray more. This world should not be left to be destroyed because of the violence by the devil, the enemy of the Cross, as Sodom and Gomorrah were destroyed despite the fervent wish by Abraham, because there were not even ten just people. Too many children are rejecting my eager pleas made with blood and joining hands with the Red Dragon, enabling him to promote errors and moral slackness among people and make them live in sins. Thus, they destroy human dignity by inducing people to commit murders through so many abortions. I implore you, because I cannot look at or listen to these anymore. (March 25, 1991)

Jesus: Too many of My children loiter around outside the door and are unable to meet Me, because they do not accept My Mother's messages of love, while insisting upon their own way of faith that they have received and are giving to others. (December 8, 1992)

My most beloved daughter! Tell all the children in the world that they should respond to the Lord's call in a hurry, if they want to be saved. How blind and deaf they are and how stubbornly they are refusing to follow me! I have been screaming until my throat bleeds, asking them to repent quickly before the cup of God's wrath, which is already filled, starts overflowing. But because so many children in the world are not listening to my words and are ignoring them, the cup of God's wrath is now beginning to overflow little by little. (February 4, 1994)

Jesus: My beloved soul! It has been ten years since My Mother Mary began shedding tears and imploring you in order to bring to Me all the children in the world who are filled with pride and hastening on their way toward hell. The Heavenly Mother, who deserves to be respected, is receiving extreme insults and pains instead of respect from the numerous children in the world. Offer up to the Heavenly Mother all of your suffering heart that has desired to comfort her. (July 1, 1995)

Jesus: Because My Mother's loving and kind words for the past several centuries have been ignored, sin has reached a saturation point, even within the Church. (September 22, 1995)

There aren't many children who are helping

Therefore, the Immaculate Heart must be made known quickly. My Heart is being torn apart and my throat is burning with thirst, but there aren't many children who are helping. Unite your efforts. My Son Jesus and I are trembling with cold, but who is giving us clothes? I feel thirsty, but who is quenching my thirst? My womb is being torn apart because of abortions, but how many have you prevented? (January 30, 1988)

Spread my messages all over the world

Tears are important, but the contents of the messages are more important. You must spread my messages fast. (October 19, 1987)

In order to help many people with prayers, sacrifices and reparations, you must get involved. I am preparing a laurel crown for you. You must be awake and pray together with my Son Jesus in Gethsemane and spread the messages all over the world. (October 19, 1987)

The Lord did not create them to become one team with the devils and, yet, they do become one and provoke God's anger. They should be sharing joy with each other in eternal love, instead. Therefore, my messages of love must spread fast for their amendment of their lives. (February 23, 1989)

Now, come closer to me with love and entrusting everything to me. Spread my messages of love vigorously to all the children so that the lost Love of God may be restored in every corner of the world. The storm is already becoming violent. I want to rescue this world into my Immaculate Heart, as it is facing the grave danger of being swept away by the storm and being destroyed. (November 11, 1990)

Therefore, all the children of the world! Open your hearts widely without delay and return to me. Rekindle the fire in your hearts that has been extinguished, achieve a unity among all and practice my messages of love. Spread the messages all over the world fervently and filled with hope. When the messages are practiced by the little souls in the form of prayers of a deep love, it will become a fragrant oil washing the bleeding wounds of the Lord. (January 29, 1991)

My beloved daughter! Spread my messages of love courageously in all the corners of the world. You will experience many difficulties, but do not forget that I am with you always. Offer up sacrifices and reparations without ceasing for the sake of my poor children. Your pains that cause bleeding inside of you will certainly not be fruitless. (May 31, 1992)

Now the plans of my Immaculate Heart are about to be realized. Therefore, help the little, unworthy soul *(Julia)* whom I have chosen and spread my wishes to the whole world so that they may be put into practice. When the messages of love that my Son Jesus and I give you are realized in this world, the greatest victory of establishing the glorious Kingdom of Christ will be won and you will see the glory by my side. (April 14, 1993)

40

In this dangerous age, so corrupt with many kinds of sins and permeated with errors, you must spread my messages of love courageously to the entire world. Console me by combining your strengths and achieving a closer unity in love among all of you and with your spiritual directors. In this age when numerous children are mired in errors and being swept away by the tides of evil without even knowing it, hurriedly bring the herds of sheep, which have been trampled upon and scattered around, to my side. I will guide them to my Son Jesus. However heinous their sins may have been, my Son Jesus will become a wonder medicine of balsam for all their wounds that have been caused by hatred, anger and sins and will save them, if they open their hearts widely and rush to Him. (January 21, 1994)

Courageously and hurriedly spread my messages of love to the whole world so that all my children may respond to the words I give them shedding tears and tears of blood and that they may repent. If you accept my words without reservation and follow Jesus in this world which is becoming more and more miserable, you will experience my presence filled with motherly love in this age of dangerous trials; this world will become purified resulting in the softening of God's just anger; the victory of my Immaculate Heart will be achieved, bringing the Lord's Kingdom into this world; and you, who are working for me, will surely stand by my side. (January 21, 1994)

Priests and children whom I have chosen! Today I will build you up like a well-defended castle and like iron pillars and brass walls. So, rapidly spread my messages of love to all the children so that they may live according to the messages. When my messages of love are practiced properly, I will bring back even those who have been taken away by the devil to the end of the earth and will sustain them forever. Then, you will be embraced and fondled in my Bosom of Love and will regain spiritual and physical vitality by drinking my milk. (August 12, 1994)

My priests and children who have been invited to my love! As I will help you with my power that can crush the serpent, spread my messages of love to the entire world with a hundredfold increase in your courage so that the messages may be practiced in everyone's life. (August 12, 1994)

These days the tricks of the devil are so deceptive and sometimes even involve supernatural phenomena. For this reason, even good souls and many shepherds are being misled taking many sheep to calamity and perdition. I ask you, whom I have called, to spread my messages of love to them and, thus, wake them up so that they may truly understand the Lord, as they are now blind and deaf spiritually and are inviting their own chastisement and walking toward their perdition. My Son Jesus spread the Good News of Salvation saving numerous souls and performing many miracles of love during His short public life. Likewise, I have prepared you for this extremely important moment. So, help all others convert, heal their illnesses, treat their deep wounds, spread the graces, peace and love, and forgive them regardless of their offenses. (September 24, 1994)

But daughter! The world is being placed in a grave danger because of the escalating sins. In this extremely important age when the cup of God's just anger is overflowing, you must display the spirit of martyrdom and hurriedly inform all the children in the world of the wishes of this anxious Mother as the final effort to save this world. The human race is going through agonizing moments at many places around the world. Members of the same family are striking each other, nations are confronting one another, and people in the same nation are cruelly killing each other. Isn't this a time of terrible sufferings? (October 23, 1994)

Spread my messages not only to Catholics but to all

Martin Luther tried the Reformation, but he, too, was a beloved son of mine just like yourselves. Humans can make mistakes, but remember that the Lord can turn evil into good and use even our mistakes. Therefore, do not ever judge and criticize others in human ways. The smaller separated churches have not accepted me, but will gradually accept me as the Mother of the Church. My beloved little souls! As I was together with the Apostles in the cenacle in Jerusalem, I will always be with you, who are following me. So, spread my words of love not only to Catholics but also to all my children in the world. You, who are spreading the words that the Lord and I give you, may experience internal death agonies; but remember that your Heavenly Mother has prepared a refuge where you can relax forever. Continue your strenuous efforts, spreading the truth about the Lord, Who is truly present in the Eucharist. (September 24, 1994)

Many are revolting against God with enormous pride

Many children are revolting against God with enormous pride, breaking their vows, and even contradicting and ridiculing His Teachings. Therefore, I ask that my messages be spread fast. (November 27, 1989)

People are not entrusting everything to my Immaculate Heart

This age is becoming too evil. Because people should entrust everything to my Immaculate Heart but are not doing so, they fall into the devil's temptations. Thus, they make preposterous errors insisting that evil is good. (November 6, 1988)

Do not speak ill of others

My little soul! However many good works you may have accumulated, they will collapse one after another if you neglect little things and speak ill of others. Be slow in opening your mouth and control your tongue wisely. When you feel like criticizing others, cover them with love. This will be a good work, too. Be holy in your words and deeds. (January 10, 1988)

Look at the children who are going toward hell by judging and criticizing others. (December 8, 1988)

Make the Passion of my Son Jesus known

I will always be with you. Do not feel lonesome, as I am always with you. So, with me, tell people about the Passion of my Son

Jesus. You must climb Mt. Calvary carrying the cross of love—with Jesus. (October 19, 1987)

Do not weep or worry for my pains, but make the Passion of Jesus known all over the world. Some priests and religious do not carry out their obligations properly and fall into sins of impurity. For this reason, Jesus is being hit by more arrows and is bleeding on His Head with more crowns of thorns. But there are no children to wipe away His Blood. (January 30, 1988)

Restore my place in the Church

Julia! Tell Father Spies. I can go back to my original place by myself, but I prefer to be placed there by the priest. I do not just mean the original place for the statue, but my original place as the Mother of the Church. I should be respected by all, but, instead, I am despised, abandoned, neglected, handled carelessly, and avoided. I feel much sadness in my Heart. Help me quickly. (February 4, 1988)

Oh, my beloved children! Too many of you are walking toward hell. Ask the Bishop to restore my position in the Church. Then, my messages will spread to the world and people will amend their lives, will be liberated from the road leading to hell, will convert and start walking on the way toward Heaven, and, thereby, will soften the just anger of God the Father. (December 8, 1988)

Julia's Sufferings

So much pain has been given to you. Your heart is pierced with a sword, stops functioning and becomes cold on the cross, which is a terrifying instrument of torture. Frightful pains that come from twisting your arms and legs (with heavy wooden sticks) and crushing your heart. Your heart becomes paralyzed because of the countless arrows. Your body is full of wounds from scourgings and becomes unmovable. Your throat becomes so dry that you cannot even swallow saliva. Your head is bleeding under the pressure from the crown of thorns. (January 30, 1988)

But I tell you again that, through such terrible pains that you suffer, the spiritually blind will see, those chained to the world will be set free and many souls imprisoned in darkness will return to the Immaculate Heart. (January 30, 1988)

So, my daughter, rejoice in your sufferings. Offer me all your pains—even the smallest ones. The burden of atonement is heavy, but I will be with you as you climb Mt. Calvary with Jesus in love. (January 30, 1988)

Even at this very moment, numerous souls are walking toward hell. I wish to save them through your sacrifices and sufferings. Will you take part in the pains? (July 24, 1988)

Thank you, my daughter! You think you are unworthy, but, as all of you are precious to me, you are also an indispensable instrument for me. (July 27, 1988)

Oh, my beloved daughter! My little soul who follows me happily even while suffering. Often you groan and get depressed under the pressure of pains, fall down with the heavy cross, and struggle to get up but cannot. Instead of getting help, a heavy rock is placed upon the cross. How painful you must be feeling! I am comforted in your heart, which anguishes even over small mistakes. (January 15, 1989)

My daughter who has to suffer pains. My Son Jesus and I are comforted, because the souls hardened like a rock are melting by your sufferings and reparations. (January 29, 1989)

I also experienced the same kind of weaknesses that you have and my human nature went through terrifying pains. That is why I love and nurture you, who is so poor. (November 26, 1989)

Do not worry too much. My Son Jesus uses an unworthy person like you and pulls you out of nothingness for His glory. Your humility in thinking that you are ignorant and unqualified is what I want. Entrust yourself completely to that grace. (November 27, 1989)

Jesus: Daughter! I feel the love of a little soul in your heart, as you think you are poor, unworthy and weak. That is why I have entrusted the work to you. So, do not worry too much. (January 26, 1993)

Jesus: Have total confidence in My Mother

Jesus: I send My Love continuously to My High Priest, the Pope, Cardinals, Bishops and priests. My Mother will help them so that My Love may flow abundantly into all the souls. Have total confidence in My Mother. (June 5, 1988)

Jesus: My Heart suffers intensely, because she receives so much pain for you and calls you again and again to spread My Love even until her throat begins to bleed, but she is not respected by her children in the world even on this great Feast of hers. Wipe away her tears of blood in a hurry with your life, consoling her with love and respecting her. (December 8, 1992)

Jesus: My beloved children! Today is the Feast commemorating My Mother Mary's Immaculate Conception in preparation for My Incarnation into this world. It was part of My Father's plan of salvation. But, as I said before, if she did not say, *"I am the handmaid of the Lord. Let it be done unto me as you say,"* My Father could not have done anything about it, as He gave her free will. Therefore, all of you must also say a humble *"Yes"* following the example of My Mother Mary. (December 8, 1992)

Jesus: Also have complete trust in and reliance on My Mother who is also your Heavenly Mother. My Mother, who is united to the sufferings of My Sacred Heart and is weeping tears and tears of blood and praying constantly so that all the children in this world may leave their sinful ways and return to My Bosom of Love, is the only one who can turn the just anger of God the Father away from you. (November 2, 1994)

Jesus: My beloved little soul! The greatest treasure in My Church is My Mother Mary who is most holy. My Mother is the Queen of the Universe, the Queen of Heaven and your Mother. Therefore, My Mother Mary can love you, as I loved you, and can do anything that I can do through the grace from Me. Today My Mother, who is the Queen of Heaven and your Mother, is opening and showing My Heart through my little and unworthy soul to the Bishop who is trying to follow Me and My Mother like an infant so that he can make it known more widely that I am truly present in the Eucharist, which is a sublime mystery of Faith and Love. (September 22, 1995)

Jesus: Hurriedly live a consecrated life, praying and offering up sacrifices and penance so that you may be connected to the Power that is indispensable for the eventual victory and, thus, do reparations for the most abominable sins of blasphemy that have been committed since early times. And if you follow My Mother Mary in order to restore My honor that has been trampled upon, you will not get lost, even in the dark maze of life in this world. My Mother Mary is the shortcut to Me, a shining dawn of My renewed Church, and the ark of a new covenant. (September 22, 1995)

Heaven—Our True Home

Countless angels were playing a beautiful and majestic symphony welcoming the souls who were entering Heaven. Also, numerous Saints were welcoming them with loud cheers. Jesus was waiting for them with open arms, and the Blessed Mother was stretching out her hands to hold them. God the Father smiled, expressing a welcome with His eyes. St. Joseph was also welcoming them.

It was a place without any jealousy or resentment. All were sharing love with one another. It was filled with love, peace and joy. It was a place of heavenly banquet where one does not become hungry even without eating.

The Blessed Mother prepared crowns of flowers and put them on people, who then danced holding each other's hands. In the flower garden, Jesus and the Blessed Mother together held up her mantle, and all were entering the inside of the mantle. All were humble to each other and were keeping order to avoid inconveniencing others. Their faces were full of smiles and were beautiful. (July 24, 1988)

Purgatory

It is a place where one must walk into the terrible flames of fire. There, one does the unfinished penance of this world and becomes purified. It is a place far away where those who die in grace but have unfinished reparations must walk the way of atonement. When they are completely purified, they are lifted into Heaven by the angels with the help of the Blessed Mother. The process can be expedited, if we in this world pray for them. We can also help them by making sacrifices and doing penance for them.

It will be too late to regret not having done penance in this world. So, while still alive in this world, one must offer love constantly through sacrifices for others. (July 24, 1988)

Hell

When the angels tie the hands of the condemned souls and drop them, the devils snatch them violently. Then, they fall into the flames of fire. It is a place of eternal perdition. It is useless, however hard one may regret and struggle. It is a sea of fire filled with hatred. Who will hold their hands? Nobody.

People struggle like a person drowning and trying to grab even a straw, but only run around in the fire, tear each other down, and try to take food away from others, but all the food burns in the fire, and nobody can eat anything. So, they are growling with eyes that are sticking out. They become horrible devils. It was a terrible scene one could not even look at. (July 24, 1988)

Many fall into the devil's temptations even after experiencing my love

Come closer to me and help me with your united strength. How numerous are the poor children who have fallen into the devil's wicked temptations even after experiencing my love. You will be encountering many difficulties while spreading my messages of love for the purpose of helping people follow the Lord. However, by spreading my messages, you will be following me and applying fragrant oil to the wounds of those who are crying and screaming in the middle of the swamps of sins. (August 12, 1994)

I am the string that ties Heaven and earth together

The string that ties Heaven and earth together is I, your Mother. My Heart suffers so much pain, because errors abound everywhere in the world and penetrate even my chosen children to an outrageous degree. (July 24, 1988)

My Son Jesus will bestow the cup of blessing on you through the loving benevolence of me, who is the string that ties Heaven and earth together. (May 8, 1990)

Our Lady sheds tears of blood through her statue in Naju.

The world will pass away, and so will all the passions. But you will surely be saved, if you hold the hands of this Mother who is the string that ties Heaven and earth together and who eagerly desires your salvation. You will live forever, if you try to live according to the Will of God. (July 21, 1990)

I am the Queen of Heaven

I should be respected as the Queen of Heaven, but I am suffering constantly because of the children on earth. (January 8, 1989)

Daughter! When I was on earth, many people called me the mother of a mad man. I should be respected as the Queen of Heaven, but have to implore with many sacrifices, pains, and tears because of the division and disorder among the children on earth. Help me. (October 4, 1990)

Jesus: My Mother is the shortcut to Me

Jesus: In this world which is being covered with errors and darkness, stay close to the Bible, which contains the Sacred Truths, lead a life according to the Gospels, and put into practice the words of My Mother who has been appearing and imploring with tears at many places in the world in this urgent time. Tell everyone that accepting My Mother's words is the same as accepting Me and that holding her hands and following her is the shortcut to Me. (May 16, 1991)

Jesus: My dear children! Listen well. Keep in mind that My Mother only leads you to a life of intense love inside My noble Heart. Come to Me hurriedly through My Mother, who is the shortcut to Me. (December 8, 1992)

Jesus: Have unshakable trust In Me

Jesus: Children! Look. The devil will try to shake your faith and trust (in Me). You should not think that such things will not happen. Enter My Sacred Heart and deepen your understanding of My Heart and My Love. Do not lose trust even briefly so that the devil may not sneak into your hearts. When you are lacking in trust, you not only hurt My Heart, but also sadden God the Father. (September 14, 1988)

Jesus: Be sure that the only way you need to walk is the way of love, a little person's way of love. Until you reach the Heavenly Kingdom by walking this way, trusting Me completely, live only for love and preserve a loving heart through sufferings, even if your sufferings may be constant. Even when you make mistakes by misusing your free will, I still love you. You know well that I will not leave you. (September 14, 1988)

Jesus: Do not worry, but follow Me with complete trust in Me. I will be with you all as I am with you now wherever you may be. When you come to Me always through Mary, My Mother, you will receive the light of blessing. (June 1, 1992)

Revitalize your faith

Daughter, look. Those numerous children are mired in sins and are provoking the just anger of God the Father. More prayers are needed. Greater sacrifices and atonement are necessary. There are too few consecrated children. Superficial prayers, visitations out of habit, service without heart, lukewarm Legio Marie activities, and so on. . . all these must be revitalized. (January 8, 1989)

I pray and suffer pains for you without ceasing

I pray and suffer pains constantly for the children who have fallen into evil habits and corruption so that fire may not fall upon the earth from the sky. But, if they refuse to accept my messages and continue accommodating to the world instead of the heavenly matters, it will be too late to regret. (January 8, 1989)

Recurring Warnings

You will be saved, if you do not ignore my tears and tears of blood, accept my words well and live a life based on the Gospels. But, if you do not, major calamities from the sky, on the ground, and in the seas will continue to happen. The world will experience all kinds of disasters. There will be moments of incredible distress in the near future. Therefore, do not think these are accidental happenings. Be awake and pray. (October 14, 1989)

Daughter! It is too hard to look at the disorder brought about by so many of my dear children in collaboration with our enemy, the Red Dragon, because of their blindness and deafness. The world is like a desert. The big calamities that occur here and there are warnings. I feel so sad and anxious, as I watch human sufferings under the warnings and punishments. Therefore, daughter! I implore you with sorrows in order to protect you from the traps laid by the devils. (March 10, 1991)

Because they are not following the Lord's Words and my messages of love, many chastising warnings are falling upon them: earthquakes, floods, droughts, traffic accidents, fires, hunger, disease, major destructions, many kinds of ecological disasters, abnormal climates. . . . Even so, they do not wake up, making my Heart burn and burn so much that I shed tears of blood. (January 23, 1993)

Therefore, all the children in the world! Come hurriedly to me so that we can go to the Lord together. Do not think that the many disasters that are occurring all over the world are just random accidents. You must wake up quickly and divert God's wrath from you. (February 4, 1994)

As I told you before, the natural order is now being disturbed and abnormalities are occurring frequently. Thousands and thousands of people are dying because of floods, fires, famines, earthquakes, droughts, tidal waves, traffic accidents, large-scale destructions, many kinds of environmental disasters, and unusual weather. Also, many people are dying because of wars, incurable illnesses and contagious diseases. When snow falls and cold wind blows, you know winter is beginning. When new buds sprout, you know it is spring. Then, why do you still not understand that these disasters are the signs of the beginning of great calamities? Through these many signs, you should know that the time of great calamities is close at hand. Those who suffer most in this world are the innocent babies who are being killed in their mothers' wombs. Why should there be such cruel, inhuman evils? (February 4, 1994)

My dear children! Many children were sacrificed *(during the earthquake in Kobe, Japan)*, not because they were at fault, but because there only were extremely few children who were accepting the Lord's Words and me. Do not think complacently of this as a matter of people far away, but pray. If you do not live according to God's Words and do not go to the Lord with me, there may be more and more natural disasters, depletion of natural resources, wars, communicable diseases, many kinds of environmental pollution, and other calamities. Therefore, you must stay awake, pray and live a life of conversion and, thereby, enter my Immaculate Heart. (January 18, 1995)

The Approaching Chastisement

You must not ignore the wrath of God. But the Lord does not wish that you avoid sins for fear of punishments. What He wants is love. (January 8, 1989)

I implore you, because punishment can come from human beings themselves *(meaning a Third World War)*. Hell is a place of terrifying and irreversible punishments, a pit of death and ruin, and a place of inextinguishable fire and maggots that will not die. Let's pray that these souls may not be condemned and all may be saved. (January 8, 1989)

Look. This world is decaying with errors. My Son Jesus is being crucified unceasingly because of the proud and cowardly pessimists and the self-righteous egoists who are habitually involved in corrupt activities and hypocritical lies. I implore you again, because the punishment can come through a Third World War. (January 29, 1989)

In order to avoid the approaching calamities, the children who have been called must climb Mt. Calvary with a deep, silent love—without sighs or lamentations, even if they are ruthlessly despised and are insulted under the heavy burden of pains. Thus, they are being crucified together with my Son Jesus for the conversion of sinners. (August 29, 1989)

Children! I beg you. Like the Israelites who crossed the Red Sea and entered the fertile land of Canaan after the slavery in Egypt, you must also leave evil, practice my messages, and, thereby, walk toward Heaven. If not, you will not be able to escape the crisis of the Third World War. It will be too late to regret. You must not forget that, as God called Moses to Mt. Sinai to save the Israelites, I am calling you without ceasing, imploring with tears in order to save you. (October 14, 1989)

What might have happened, if Noah did not say "Yes" and obey, when Yahweh told him to build a ship to save him? Keep in your heart my words spoken with tears of blood. How can you be so blind and deaf? My Heart is flaming up intensely, because families, the Church and society are becoming corrupt and the politicians are unable to achieve unity. Quickly renounce yourselves and come to me. (October 14, 1989)

If I did not help you, the world would have become seas of fire already. But I will never leave you. Therefore, open your ears when you hear precious words and close your ears when you hear slanders. Even when you walk in darkness, follow me with confidence. Your sighs will turn into joys, if you accept my messages well and practice them. (October 14, 1989)

Their sins are many, but I have pity on them and wait for their return. But, if they persist in being indifferent to me and rejecting me, God's arm of justice will soon be raised and the cup of His wrath will overflow. What will be the use of regretting at that time? (August 15, 1990)

Major calamities are about to fall upon the world, but there are too many people who are self-centered. Those who love God and make me known will receive eternal life and will stand by the side of this Mother of Love. The world will change, but the Laws of God will not. Pray and pray again. Prayers of deep love are needed now more than ever for the Holy Catholic Church. This current age is extremely important for the whole human race. (October 4, 1990)

Follow me with courage even when faced with serious tribulations and threats of violence, wars and destruction. There isn't much time left before incredible punishments will fall even upon those countries which have been protected and intensely cherished so far. Many people are inordinately rejecting God, and the iniquities and corruptions are increasing everyday, causing more violence and more wars. (January 29, 1991)

If you do not reject my motherly love and practice love, my Immaculate Heart will achieve a victory in the face of the threat of a new, terrifying war, and there will be love and peace in the world. I will stretch and open my mantle and hide and save in the safe refuge of my Immaculate Heart all those souls who follow my words even in the midst of a huge darkness. But those who do not accept my words and reject the Lord will be thrown into the sea of an intense fire. Therefore, have trust in me, the Mother of Peace, and rely completely on my Immaculate Heart. (January 29, 1991)

All the children of the world! How sad it will be if the fire falls upon you from the sky! Pray and pray again. This current age is extremely important for the whole human race. Shouldn't you find ways to protect yourselves from the many calamities? Your God looks down at your acts and is about to punish you. But He is still forgiving you. Repent hurriedly. Repent sincerely and come back to God Who can save you. You must repent, because the sins of this world have reached an extremely high level. The world is mired in evil habits and delinquency. As order is disturbed, chaos is increasing, and the spiritual world is being destroyed. All things are collapsing, provoking the wrath of God. (March 10, 1991)

My beloved children! Become little persons and follow me humbly and with hope and courage. When you follow me wholeheartedly in response to my messages of love, new buds will sprout even from the burnt ground, my love will flame up on the ruins, and a cup of blessing instead of a cup of wrath will be bestowed upon you by God. (March 10, 1991)

Do not worry, but follow me with full trust in me. The Lord will rebuild upon the destruction by the devil and will cure the wounds. The world is going against me, offending me, striking me and hurting me, but there are faithful little souls who are praying by my side. Therefore, combine your prayers and achieve unity. When fervent prayers of poor souls reach Heaven, God's just anger will be appeased. Pray and pray again. (August 27, 1991)

Children! All the souls reaching the Bosom of God will enjoy eternal love, peace and joy in the Lord's Love. But those who betray the graces, are ungrateful and insult the Holy Spirit will be cut off from the Lord forever. (September 17, 1991)

Jesus: My Mother prepares a safe refuge in her Immaculate Heart for all of you and leads you to Me. The hour of the pains and chastisement of Gethsemane and Calvary is approaching the children of the world. But the gate to Heaven will open through the prayers, graceful consecrations and bloody efforts by you, My little children. Do not fear. Entrust everything to Me with faith and trust. I will be with you always. (December 8, 1992)

Daughter! Let's pray more fervently for the human race which is bringing about its own destruction and for the Church and the Pope. The whole human race must convert in a hurry, before it cries out in fear. (January 23, 1993)

As nobody knows the time of the Lord's Coming, no one knows when God will take your soul. Therefore, stay awake with love, praying with me. If you accept the Lord's Words and me well, you will see even greater miracles in my garden and enjoy eternal life in the Lord's Kingdom of Love. (February 6, 1993)

All the children in the world! My beloved sons and daughters! Do not bring about the chastisement of darkness, fire and blood upon you. People were eating, drinking and marrying until the very day Noah was entering the Ark. They were all swept away by the flood. If you do not listen to my voice with which I am imploring you so ardently, you will be putting yourselves in the same situation. (February 4, 1994)

My beloved children! Didn't I tell you that, when the sounds of prayers by little souls are combined together and soar high into Heaven, the cup of blessing instead of chastisement will be bestowed upon you? Now, I want to combine all of your prayers, sacrifices, penance, consecration, self-denial, poverty and sufferings together, put them in the cup of my Immaculate Heart, and offer them up to God's Justice that demands reparations. (February 4, 1994)

God can pluck, tear down, demolish and destroy (what stands in this world), but wills to shorten this time of internal death agony by using you as His instruments chosen by me to apply fragrant oil to the wounds of those who need your help while wandering on their sinful roads in this dangerous age. (August 12, 1994)

As I told you before, daughter, fire can fall from the sky upon the souls who are blind and deaf and are wandering without knowing the way. But there are not enough little souls yet who can soften the just anger of God. Therefore, help me by moving to the place which I have prepared *(the mountain where the new basilica will be built)*, holding hands with the priests whom I have chosen with love. (February 2, 1995)

The time when God the Father will speak with a stern voice of judgment is approaching. You must protect yourselves with prayers, sacrifices, penance and consecration. My Heart has already been torn apart into pieces, and my bloody tears and bloody sweat are pouring down on the earth. (June 18, 1995)

I have already told you that the terrifying judgment of God will come down. As you know, that day will come like a thief at night. Destruction will come suddenly, when people are singing of peaceful and secure times. It will be like the pains of delivery to a pregnant woman, which are sudden and yet certain and cannot be avoided. The souls who accept my messages that you are spreading are accepting me. Those who reject them reject me and reject the Father in Heaven. (June 18, 1995)

Already, the time for preparation is over and, now, you are entering the decisive time of battle. The human race will face the time of a great bloody chastisement. Shouldn't you rescue (people) hurriedly? Do not delay, but hurry up. This Mother in Heaven is trying to save even one more soul. Why are you calculating and thinking in human ways? (June 19, 1995)

I ask all the children who work for the Lord and help me. For the conversion of sinners, pray, offer sacrifices, do penance and live a consecrated life. Turn your life into prayers. The human race has already come to the brink of a cliff of destruction because of its degradation. The ongoing battles are the signs of the approaching great chastisement that will befall the human race. From now on, how many countries will be turned upside down and how many people will have to be sacrificed. . . . If those who pursue evil persist in contradicting God the Father's Will, how can I continue preventing His Hand of Justice (from striking)? (June 21, 1995)

The Devil's Violence

As you approach God more fervently in order to bear fruit, the devils will intensify their attacks on you, and they will become more active to prevent you from bearing fruit. (January 15, 1989)

Satan wants to overthrow my Church and destroy life in the souls. But, when you fight against him holding a shield of love, his true character will be revealed. (January 29, 1989)

Do not fear. When you feel uneasy, the devils will intensify their attacks and work harder to achieve their victory. They are becoming more active, employing all kinds of methods to defeat you, as many souls get to see the light thanks to the grace of conversion through your sacrifices and sufferings. (February 23, 1989)

The vicious devils are even penetrating the inside of the Church causing division, confusion and darkness. How serious the harms to the sheep will be! Therefore, daughter, pray, make sacrifices and do penance with a greater love in this time of darkness. (August 29, 1989)

What a dear price has to be paid to defeat the devil! I feel anxious when I see you. Daughter! Take courage and offer up your sufferings more gracefully. Also pray harder for unity. As my messages are spreading to the world and are being put into practice, the devils are becoming more and more active. The Red Dragon is employing all kinds of means to promote division, even among priests. Make our enemy, Satan, powerless with your faith and love. By doing so, help me save many souls. Offer to me even what you think is miserable. My motherly Heart gets wounded, as I watch all this. (May 8, 1990)

Right now, the devil is using all kinds of methods to defeat you and to strike down priests and many children whom I have chosen so that the messages may not spread. The flowers of evil look pretty on the exterior and confuse and seize even innocent souls in cunning ways. Such evils hide even behind innocent-looking appearances. This can be discerned only by the souls who are in the state of grace. Can you offer sufferings, if these sufferings are needed for the proud and selfish souls who claim to know the ways of Heaven and sound very knowledgeable, but do not put what they know into practice? (August 15, 1990)

All the children of the world! Darkness can never defeat light. The devils are trying to strike down many of my children who are following me. But do not forget that the Lord does not refuse the pleas of those who call upon His Name with love and follow me. (April 21, 1991)

Satan is striving with all his power to promote a tendency of despising the Holy Laws of the Lord, but my burning Immaculate Heart will achieve victory, when the sounds of little souls' prayers to my Immaculate Heart soar high to Heaven. You will surely see my victory. (September 17, 1991)

I am your Mother who has been elevated to Heaven. Because the devil knows well that I came to this world to help you, he is becoming more active, employing all the available methods to alienate you from me, the Mother of Love, and attacking you fanatically using all kinds of cunning schemes. But the Lord intends to advance the date of purification to separate good and evil in response to the prayers by the little souls who are working for the Lord and following me. (October 19, 1991)

Because people join forces with the devil through their pride, they, even without realizing themselves, become wolves that wear sheepskin and plunder habitually and drive numerous sheep mercilessly into a whirlpool of confusion. (May 27, 1993)

At this time when the devils are trying to conquer the whole world, I am calling you so that we can confront them together. So, I want you to offer yourselves up well. When you help my little soul who works for me, you are helping me. (January 21, 1994)

Daughter! My messages of love that I am giving through you, who is unworthy, can be a guide for all the souls. But because only very few are following them, big calamities that Satan wants and is causing are occurring repeatedly. God has not taken away the devils' abilities that they were created with.

That is why they proudly came to the world and are reigning. They lead people to sins, instigate them to disobey God, infuse pride, which is a terrible vice, into them and constantly plan evil schemes. Their hypocrisy and malice become combined together and become like a mixture of explosive gases, making the spiritual warfare more fierce. You will not even be able to discern, unless you remain awake. (July 2, 1995)

In this period of purification, the devils, my enemies, are mobilizing all kinds of deceptions, even showing many supernatural phenomena and miracle-like occurrences. This way, they are misleading not only the innocent and good-willed souls, but also some priests and religious by instigating their curiosity and making them believe (the deceptions), bringing about confusion. (November 21, 1995)

The devil, the enemy, is confident that he has already won the victory in the Church. But, as I am always with you, I, your Heavenly Mother, will offer up the Pope, who is the first son of the Church, and you (plural) to the Lord's temple as (I did to) my Baby Jesus and will pour down the fragrant oil of balsam upon your heads so that you may be saved, if you walk the way of spiritual childhood and reform your lives humbly and as little persons according to the teachings in the Gospels and my messages of love. (January 6, 1996)

Many shepherds are facing the danger of losing true faith

Jesus: Many shepherds may appear to have faith in Me, but their souls are closed and locked and do not truly accept Me. When they celebrate Mass in a superficial way, they are closing the door to God, while opening it to the devil. Thus, the devil is causing confusion even among the shepherds and is making them become insensitive to and unaware of their sins and is making them become defenseless. Because of this, numerous children who say they are believers are treating the Eucharist carelessly. How can I work in them? (November 2, 1994)

Daughter! My enemy's fury is increasing rapidly and he is crying out with joy and victoriously over the fall of many priests. This Mother of Heaven cannot help weeping continuously because of the heretics who have deviated from the true and traditional Church. Many priests, who should look after the sheep which have been lost and are wandering about, are facing the danger of losing true faith. They even sometimes forget about the Resurrection of Jesus, because they are immersed in the spirit of the world which is permeated with disbelief and errors. Thus, the tide of a great apostasy is spreading extensively inside the Catholic Church. Therefore, try to become signs of my love filled with my Motherhood. . . . (May 9, 1995)

Jesus: I have shown signs several times through my little soul to enlighten the many priests and numerous other children who say that they know My Real Presence and My breathing in the Eucharist with My Body, Blood, Soul and Divinity, and yet do not really know it. But only very few children are following Me. Even many priests forget about the sublime simplicity of the Holy Eucharist, which is My Physical Presence, and of the Gospels which I teach, and they are trying to spread Me with deceptive talks and complicated reasonings. This is like throwing mud at simple people. (September 22, 1995)

You are in a spiritual war

Now is the time for a huge battle between me and my enemy. Our enemy is the army of the Red Dragon, who looks like a terrible animal. All the devils are out to conquer this earth from hell. They are challenging to corrupt many souls of this world by making them reject God, commit sins with all kinds of selfishness and defile everything. Thereby, they are trying to form an army. (August 26, 1989)

A huge battle has begun already. Since it is a spiritual war, arm yourselves with me by entrusting everything to my Immaculate Heart. Also practice the messages of my love. Then, you will be able to escape from the terrible chastisement approaching the human race and the Church. (August 26, 1989)

Prepare a tabernacle in the Chapel

My Son Jesus is shedding blood and sweat. Too many souls are joining their forces with the devils. Therefore, prepare a tabernacle in the Chapel so that we can pray with my Son Jesus. Then, there will certainly be a victory. Help me. Invite my Son Jesus in, Who will shine brightly in this dark world. (February 23, 1989)

My beloved daughter! I have a request to the representative of the Pope, my son, whom I love so dearly that I can put him in my eyes without feeling any pain. Ask him that a tabernacle be prepared beside me. (November 24, 1994)

Jesus: My Mother has repeatedly asked for a tabernacle to be prepared (in the Chapel). But because it has not been prepared yet, I am giving you today My Flesh and My Blood in a special way for all of you. (July 1, 1995)

I will help you by amazing methods in an invisible way

My beloved children! Even if you suffer from persecutions and pains that are beyond imagination, I will help you at your side by amazing methods and will carry through my plan to the end and accomplish it. The devil will afflict you with violent and persistent attacks, but I am protecting you at your side from the devil in an invisible way to accomplish my plan. I will protect you; so, stay awake. When you confront the devil and lead many souls to my Immaculate Heart, you are leading them to my Son Jesus. This will become the most beautiful floral crown of glory in my Immaculate Heart. (January 21, 1994)

Pray for the Pope and follow him

Leave everything to me and do not be anxious to know the end results. Pray and offer sacrifices and reparations constantly for the Pope, Cardinals, Bishops and priests. Those who are being controlled by the devils are trying hard to strike down the Holy Father and lead the Church to destruction. But all the devils will lose power, when my tears and blood are combined with your sacrifices and reparations. (October 14, 1989)

Jesus: When you feel humble and weak, you resemble My Mother. Now, pray harder for the Pope. He always stands alone on Calvary, tired and lonesome. He is My Father's beloved son, Peter's successor and my Vicar whom I have chosen. My enemies are becoming more active by employing all the available means to topple him. All of you must display the power of love by following him and uniting with him in prayer and loyalty and sharing his cross, as the devil is planning violent attacks on him by deceiving humans in cunning ways through those who are close to them and, thereby, making them disobey the Pope, who is the shepherd of the whole world. (January 26, 1993)

Daughter! My Son Jesus gave Peter the Keys of Heaven. Isn't the Pope the successor of Peter? Pray and offer sacrifices for the Pope. Support and protect him. As the Vicar of My Son Jesus, he is carrying a heavy cross. He has been consecrated to me, loves me so much and accepts me so well. . . . He already understands my words that I am giving to all with tears and tears of blood in Korea. (June 27, 1993)

To the Pope, who is my son, whom I love without limit and whom I can put in my eyes without feeling any pain, I will give a special love and sign. (June 27, 1993)

The Pope, who is the Vicar of my Son Jesus and the first son of the Church, is groaning under the death agony at Gethsemane at this time. His heart is being pressed down with deep sorrows, as he climbs Mt. Calvary carrying a cross of cruel pains. As he is human, he suffers from the weakening of his body and the pains and fatigue in his body. But he feels more pains and a deep loneliness, because many, who used to support him and love him dearly, are betraying him like Judas, disobeying him, blocking him and not supporting him any more. However, I am always supporting him at his side with my motherly love. Therefore, you must remain loyal to him, support and protect him, listen to his words, be united with him and pray for him continuously with a loving heart. (October 23, 1994)

Pray in a hurry, because the devils are being extremely violent to strike you down. The Pope, who is the Vicar of my Son, the first son of the Church, and my beloved son, is now exhausted with internal and external pains. But ask him not to worry, but to entrust everything to this Heavenly Mother, as I am

shining the light that emanates from my Immaculate Heart upon him. I have already clothed him with a garment of virtues and protected and nurtured him so that everything he does in his life may be attracted to my fragrance. The purpose is to protect him and become his shield, armor and iron covering at every decisive moment so that I may lead him to the Heavenly Paradise. Therefore, all of you must become people who are closest to the Pope's heart. Listen carefully to the words he says while walking on the difficult road of the cross of Calvary and put his teachings into practice and spread them. Also help everyone to love the Pope with a filial love so that all may carry his painful cross with him. (October 27, 1995)

How many priests are willing to walk with the Pope on the road from Bethlehem to Calvary that my Son Jesus walked? Many priests are studying the teachings of the Church superficially, without depth, and behave accordingly. That is why my son, the Pope, is suffering even more. (October 27, 1995)

I feel so anxious that I wish to spread the messages of love from my burning Immaculate Heart all over the world through the Pope, who is the first son and head of the Church. Help me in a hurry. Take numerous souls, who have lost their way and are rushing toward hell, on board Mary's Ark of Salvation, which I have prepared, and guide them to Heaven. (October 27, 1995)

I wish to let the Church know through the Pope, the first son of the Church, about the protection by this Mother and about the great breadth of my Motherly Love for my children. (November 21, 1995)

To the Pope

My beloved son! Thanks to your faithful love with which you have responded to this Heavenly Mother saying *"Amen,"* no one will be able to separate you from the Love of God or take you away from Him. Your name has already been written in my Immaculate Heart. Therefore, be happy even in the middle of misunderstanding and persecution. Whenever you were in difficulties of various kinds, I defended and helped you and encouraged and consoled you in the refuge of my mantle. (October 31, 1995)

You are my beloved son whom I can put in my eyes without feeling any pain. You are my beloved first son of the Church and younger brother of Jesus. I have led you to participate in the eternal priesthood together with Jesus. Therefore, sing of the Resurrection, living a life of intimacy with Him. Then, you will become the Light of Jesus Christ that comes down through you *(plural)* shining brightly upon the world, penetrating the curtain of darkness that surrounds the world, and you will face the Second Pentecost. (October 31, 1995)

Beware of false prophets

Today, even my children in the Church are experiencing confusion because of the false prophets. Priests, who represent my Son, Jesus Christ, must be discreet and do their best to lead a life based on the teachings in the Gospels and within the orders of the Church. (October 14, 1989)

My beloved children! Listen well. I implore you. Now is the time for purification, but many children are confused because of the words that are not from God. My enemy, the devil, is promoting confusion and division at many places in the world by deceiving people with tricks and even by using supernatural phenomena. He performs many unusual tricks that can confuse even the good people. To promptly recognize the devil's violence in his attempts and to come to the refuge of my Immaculate Heart, you must build the Basilica of Mary's Ark of Salvation fast. Help me. (August 27, 1991)

How numerous are false prophets these days! They have fallen into the devil's deception and are spreading all kinds of untrue information as messages from me. That way, they are confusing my children and promoting disorder to neutralize and dilute my messages. This causes me much pain. You are also being persecuted and criticized with so many preposterous accusations. Despite such misunderstanding, have no fear, but follow me, entrusting everything to me. (January 23, 1993)

In this time of purification, so many children forget about the graces they have received, listen to the false testimonies concocted by Satan, are sidetracked from my way, and judge, criticize and condemn it. Because Satan is employing all the available means like false testimonies and even some supernatural phenomena, even many innocent people are being misled. (January 21, 1994)

Jesus: This world has become one which is swarming with heretics. In this age which is placed in the middle of a danger, try to imitate Me. (July 1, 1995)

Church approval is necessary

Since the world is still far from the truth and conversion, my voice can spread more forcefully to the world, sinners can repent, the chained people can be freed and peace can prevail, only if the Church approves my voice. (November 27, 1989)

When my messages are accepted by the Church and put into practice, the just anger of God the Father will be softened, order and truth will be restored, and the devils, who instigate confusion and cause turmoil, will be defeated. But, if the world rejects my words and refuses to repent, the fire of God's justice will fall upon the world. (November 27, 1989)

It is urgent that people put the messages into practice. But prayers are lacking. If the approval can be obtained soon, many children walking toward hell will change their course. It will also become a shortcut to world peace. (December 11, 1987)

I am asking for help from the Bishop whom I chose with love in order to wash away the stains of sinners with my tears that flow endlessly like a river, even when they are not visible. When my Son Jesus came to the children of the world because of His Love, even to the extent of becoming their Food, He came through the priests, as He wanted to obey them. In the same manner, I want to spread my increasingly anxious voice to the world through the Bishop. Please follow my wish. (November 27, 1989)

Daughter! You must unite with my son, the Bishop, and with your spiritual director. Obey them, entrust all to them and follow their guidance. They will surely receive the laurel crown from me. If they accept my words well, my Immaculate Heart will flame up with love and the world will convert and be saved. (November 27, 1989)

Love this Mother wholeheartedly

I love you despite your weaknesses. I want you to love me wholeheartedly. (June 29, 1987)

Give alms to this Heavenly Beggar, who is waiting for you, calling you and longing for you. (August 11, 1987)

Please do not leave me as a lonesome Mother. I have called and saved so many souls with my tears of mercy, but how many have followed me in gratitude for that love? (May 8, 1990)

I am sad. So many of my poor children, who are usually forgetful of me, seek me only during hard times, as if trying to grab a life buoy. . . . How can I work in such changeable hearts? (May 8, 1990)

Daughter! Thank you. I rejoice more over a heart filled with love and devotion than over flowers or deeds. Even the smallest thing can become a great good work for you, if it is done with love. Come closer to me so that you can unite more intimately with my burning love. To soften God's anger, become an even lowlier person. Become a more humble person, offering sacrifices and reparations of the cross, and entrust all your imperfect thoughts, daily life and sufferings to me. Those souls who are accepting me with love and are approaching me will be bathed in my love. Follow without a doubt the wishes of this Mommy who wants to perform miracles of love by using you as an instrument, despite your unworthiness. (May 8, 1991)

Do not forget the graces you have received

Once they receive the grace they have asked for, they return to their miserable lives, forget about my love and live in a despicable, ungrateful way. But, my daughter, my mercy prompts me to call them again. I am shedding tears of blood like this because of the poor children who are ungrateful for the blessings they have received, do not give love to others, and think that the graces they have received are their own and something that they were going to receive anyhow for their own merit. Comfort my Immaculate Heart that is suffering. (May 8, 1990)

I am Christ's Helper in Redemption

Follow me, the Mother and the Helper in Redemption, entrusting everything to my immensely wide Immaculate Heart. Do not forget that I, Mother Mary, am preparing a home where you can relax. Follow me without being discouraged. I bestow the same merciful grace on all the souls who trust and follow me and testify for me. (May 8, 1990)

Jesus: The time of my Mother Mary's victory is approaching. Make haste in repenting and get on board Mary's Ark of Salvation. My Mother came into this world as the Heavenly Prophetess and My Helper who will lead you to My brilliant and glorious revelations. Follow her words. I will always be with you. (May 16, 1991)

I came to this world as the Lord's Helper to save you in this age fallen into danger. When you renounce everything and follow me completely, my role as your true Mother and the Lord's Helper in saving the world will soon be manifested clearly. (August 27, 1991)

The reason why I was chosen to be the Lord's Helper was to give the opportunity of salvation to everyone. Keep in mind that you were also chosen to be my helpers. Accept my words well so that all may be saved together. Offer yourselves up completely, remembering my Son, Jesus Christ, Who was offered as a living sacrifice. I will give you the garment of my fragrance with the love of my burning Immaculate Heart. (August 27, 1991)

Wear the scapular

My beloved daughter! Tell all the children of the world. I want all of you to wear the scapular with the intention of being with me; pray the rosary fervently with all your body and mind and with love; live a completely consecrated life of prayers, sacrifices, and reparations; renew your life with the spirit of self-renunciation and poverty; and, thus, repel the violence of the devil. (April 21, 1991)

Observe the First Saturdays

When you observe the First Saturdays and spend the nights praying with me for the salvation of the world and enter through the small gate carrying the cross in unity, the devils will retreat and sinners will receive the grace of conversion. (July 21, 1990)

My dear children! There are many children who observe First Saturdays and yet do not know the reason for doing so. Therefore, I want to tell you today the reason for observing First Saturdays.

It was a day of cruel suffering for me—a long, long day when I was left alone, having lost my Son Jesus. I always had sufferings from the day I conceived Jesus my Son, but, on that Holy Saturday, I expressed sorrows externally for the first time and cried so miserably all night praying for my Son Jesus and for sinners. Those painful hours were also the time for transition from my Son's Death to His Resurrection, a day for going from death to life. This is the reason why I asked you to pray with me tonight. (February 6, 1993)

This Mother, who loves you all and loves especially those children who pray with me on First Saturdays, will stay with you always, as I was with the Apostles, praying with them in the Cenacle in Jerusalem, and will feed you my spiritual milk of love. Those of my children who accept me and drink the spiritual milk will receive the grace of repentance and will find peace and a great comfort in my love, and, thus, will be able to withstand any difficulties. (February 6, 1993)

If you continue observing First Saturdays well and put what I have requested of you into practice, this Mother, who is the Mediatrix, will acquire all the graces for you that you ask for, will give you a special protection and the grace needed for eternal salvation at the time of your death, take you to the Heavenly Harbor in Mary's Ark of Salvation and offer you to the Lord. (February 6, 1993)

So, on First Saturdays, unite with the Lord by making a sincere Confession, attending Holy Mass and receiving Holy Communion; approach the Sacred Bible and contemplate on the Gospels; with love, do reparations for the betrayals that have hurt the Lord's Heart; consecrate yourselves to my Immaculate Heart; pray the rosary sincerely and fervently, meditating on its Mysteries; accept everything with complete trust, humility and meekness; and live as a little person in my burning Immaculate Heart. (February 6, 1993)

Construct a Basilica

Therefore, build the Basilica of Mary's Ark of Salvation hurriedly. If you follow my messages of love and put them into practice, great treasures will accumulate for other souls and yours. It will also be the way of saving the souls who would otherwise be lost with certainty. To the burning Sacred Heart of Jesus and my Immaculate Heart, it will become a comfort. (May 8, 1991)

Oh, my beloved children! Thank you so much for offering yourselves totally. But many children are dispersing. To assemble them again with the love of my Immaculate Heart, you must build the Basilica in a hurry. Make haste with faithful hearts. I, who am the Helper in Redemption, sincerely wish that all the dispersed children repent, become purified and offer themselves up with sacrifices and reparation. Then, I will make you the Lord's glorious garlands of flowers. (August 27, 1991)

Let's brighten the road ahead together with this Mother of Love for the souls who are falling into temptations. For that purpose, build the Basilica of Mary's Ark of Salvation by joining hands together. There, I will reveal the secrets of my Immaculate Heart to you so that it may become a sign of joy, love and peace to everyone who visits it. (November 4, 1991)

If you believe that good seeds will bear fruit hundredfold and work entrusting everything to my Immaculate Heart, the Basilica of Mary's Ark of Salvation will be built. You must really hurry. This is because we need to turn even one more soul, who is falling into wars, greed, and selfishness, away from the way of hell to the just way of God. If you follow me with complete trust in me, you will have the key to my Immaculate Heart. (November 28, 1991)

My beloved daughter! Why do you hesitate at this hour when you should enter the battle? God's mercy will take root at this fertile place, which will be prepared with love, and accomplish miracles of love through you, my children. Therefore, hurriedly invite Fr. Spies and Fr. Chang, who have accepted my call, to the mountain chosen through you. Following the Will of God, Who gave you free will, I am going to make that place a shrine of mine and wash numerous souls who are walking toward hell. (May 27, 1993)

Many people are neglecting me

I am Mother to all of you and the Queen of Heaven. I have called many priests in order to save the souls who are wandering in darkness. But they have neglected me and distanced me because of the eyes of the world and face-saving. . . . (April 14, 1993)

I feel so lonely, because many leaders are ignoring me for the sake of face-saving and the eyes of the world, paying no attention to my ardent request to look after numerous sheep that are walking toward hell. (November 24, 1994)

Even many of the leaders in the Church are rejecting my messages of love and committing the sins of sacrilege by concocting many lies for the simple reason that my messages have not yet been approved. How great the damage will be to the sheep that are following them! Help me so that my messages of love may be approved soon. By doing so, you will be comforting the Lord Who is present in the Holy Eucharist. (November 24, 1994)

How numerous are the clergy who do not defend truth but keep silent for fear and remain as spectators because of face-saving and the eyes of others, even when they see errors and despite my messages of love that I have been screaming (to you) until my throat bleeds! (October 31, 1995)

From Korea, my love and victory will spread to the entire world

My beloved children! Follow me without worrying. The Lord, Who is listening to you because He wants to help you, will bestow His Love on you. When you follow me, believing my words completely, everything will be accomplished. From Korea, which is my youngest child and which I love so much, I will make my love and victory spread to the entire world. (September 17, 1991)

From this small land, a land made fertile with the blood of so many martyrs, the light will shine upon the whole world through my little, poor souls. My Immaculate Heart will surely triumph in the midst of the glorious victory by Christ. (November 4, 1991)

All the children in the world! It is not too late yet. Accept my messages of love that I give you through my little soul and come back to my bosom which will be your refuge. As I told you before, I will let the triumph of my Immaculate Heart and the light of mercy spread to the entire world from Korea. Let all the children in the world know this so that they may wake up and pray. (January 18, 1995)

The victory of my Immaculate Heart is near

I wish to rescue the world by the victory of my mercy and love. Therefore, if you pray with me, with confidence in me, holding my hands, my Immaculate Heart will triumph. It will surely triumph. (January 15, 1989)

Now, daughter! Cry out. The victory of my Immaculate Heart is close at hand. You will soon see the day when I will, through you who are unworthy, convert the children who do not know me, open the eyes of the people who do not believe, and silence those who criticize. (September 17, 1991)

Soon it will become the Age of the Apostles of the Sacred Heart of Jesus and my Immaculate Heart. At that time, there will be many who will regret and wail. Therefore, make haste. The souls who follow the Lord carrying the Cross, spread and practice the Gospels and accept the messages of my burning love will be saved and enjoy eternal life. (October 19, 1991)

My beloved little souls! The sun is light. The Lord Who came as Light is shedding light on you by opening Heaven. These signs from Heaven signify the Mystery of Salvation. They also mean that the Lord is with you and is blessing you and this land. It means that my victory is being accomplished in you, who obey me in a simple way, on this land of love illuminated by the Lord's Light according to God's Will. This way, the darkness of evil permeated with errors, with selfishness that prevents your self-renunciation, with passions and with all kinds of sins and uncleanness will be driven out. (December 5, 1991)

My dear children! The glorious day of victory for my Son Jesus is approaching in the midst of the Sacred Love of Mercy. For this reason, the heavenly light will become brighter day by day through you who have responded to me. Trust me completely and unite with each other to save the world. (December 5, 1991)

As I said before, I will build where Satan has destroyed, heal where Satan has hurt, and achieve victory where Satan appears to have won. This word of mine will surely be accomplished. For that purpose, I need your help so urgently. (August 15, 1994)

If you follow me completely, you will soon see the day when the darkness that is covering the Church will disappear. The light of love from the most merciful and loving Sacred Heart of Jesus and my Immaculate Heart is bestowed upon you so that peace instead of suffering and anxiety may be given to you. In this desolate world, the danger of a new war is turning into a reality. But the power of God's Love cannot be blocked. (June 30, 1995)

On that road, you will meet the Divine Person of my Son Jesus. And the powerful action of the Holy Spirit, my Spouse of Love, will proceed actively inside you so that all those who have lost their way and are wandering because of errors and sins may repent and that this world may face the time of the triumph of my Immaculate Heart that will blossom like a fragrant flower. (October 27, 1995)

Drink from the Miraculous Spring

Dig a spring here so that children from all over the world may drink from it. I will call the children from all over the world to wash away the dirt from their souls and bodies. Because I do not want even one soul to be condemned and go to hell, I will invite all to come and drink from the Miraculous Spring of Mary's Ark of Salvation in order to convert even the most evil sinners. Make haste. While the world is rushing into moral decay, all the children of the world will soon know that I am the Mediatrix of Graces. (November 26, 1991)

Now, I will ask the Lord to give you a miraculous spring here so that I may wash your soul and body. Soon this place will become a kingdom of love and a place of salvation under the combination of the Sacred Heart of Jesus and my Immaculate Heart, an equivalent of which will be hard to find anywhere else in the world. Soon there will be continuous rays of light coming from the Sacred Heart of Jesus and my Immaculate Heart here. People will smell the fragrance of roses and drink the water of eternal life from the Miraculous Spring. I will let all stay in my love. (November 28, 1991)

Respond to my call

But however eagerly I may call you, it will be of no use, if you do not respond, as the Lord gave you free will. The beloved children who respond to the Lord's call will enjoy eternal heavenly happiness and will be given a beautiful garment of Sanctifying Grace. Stay awake and pray, following the Lord Who offered the most noble sacrifices for us. Those who are walking proudly will soon bow their heads and become more respectful, following your example. (November 28, 1991)

What will be the use of regretting at the time of chastisement? Now is the designated hour for you and the time to enter the battle. Do not worry about tomorrow or be concerned about the future in human ways. When you humbly walk a little person's way of love toward holy virtues according to my wishes and follow me in obedience, the Lord's miracles of love will be wrought through you. (April 14, 1993)

If the children in this world do not wake up and do not accept my earnest requests, God can take away His favors from them, as He did from King Saul when he misused his free will. However, I prayed to God not to remove His Love from those who have responded to my call and are following me. So, follow me without worrying. As God did not forsake Moses, He will not abandon you. (August 12, 1994)

Jesus: I am the light of love that repels darkness

Jesus: I am Light. I am the Light of Love that chases away all the darkness. I intend to let all of you receive my Light of Love and, thus, to repel the darkness from this world that is turning into a vast desert. (June 2, 1992)

The Apostasy

There will be persecutions, as the Church gets wounded and divided, but offer up this hour of death agony well. I want all of you to stay in warm kindness to each other and in prayers of deep silence. (January 23, 1993)

Daughter! I am always with you. Why are you so worried? The devil is so violent that he is even mobilizing some of my priests in driving my messages into a whirlpool of confusion. For this reason, a terrible danger is pressing down upon the world, and the hour of apostasy and betrayal is drawing near. The degradation of the human race is worsening every day and the world is standing on the edge of a cliff. Humans are bringing about their own destruction. (January 23, 1993)

(You have already seen) internecine conflicts and major events that have changed the world drastically. Freemasonry is leading this cruel world to destruction and, by spreading heresies in the Church, is causing division and confusion and is promoting a major apostasy in the Church. Meanwhile, some Bishops, priests, religious and many lay people are leading sinful lives, having been trapped in the snares laid by the cunning and wicked Satan, and yet do not realize that they are in sins. They are walking toward hell, thinking that what they are doing is good and of true value. They are totally ignorant about this, because they are not awake. This is why my Heart has been burning so intensely that it is gushing out blood. (February 4, 1994)

This world, filled with sins and covered with darkness, is approaching destruction through many kinds of disasters and loss of faith. The activities of the Church also are becoming paralyzed because of the Freemasons. Many children and even the majority of the shepherds who set out to work for the Lord are not awake, see the things of this world from a human standpoint, and carry out their activities in a superficial way. How great the harms to the sheep who are following them will be! I am trying to warn you, who are responding to my call, that the moment of death is drawing near because of their apostasy and disloyalty and to ask for your help. (August 15, 1994)

My beloved children! The hour of apostasy and betrayal in the Church is seriously approaching, due to the work of the Freemasons, but even many of the clergy and religious are spiritually blind and deaf, are not faithful to their vocations, become corrupt internally, and do not recognize my words. This Mother feels so anxious. (October 23, 1994)

So many priests are offering Mass unfaithfully. As a result, the Lord is unable to perform miracles of love in them through His Real Presence. He is suffering pains and is unceasingly calling the priests who are in sins to be faithful to their duties and become united with the Lord's Love. (November 24, 1994)

Nowadays, errors are being taught even by some of my priests and are spreading all over the world. The Gospels are being promulgated by false prophets in such a way that the Gospels might become more acceptable to modern society under the pretext of civilization and innovation. But these are being promoted unfaithfully and are not the Gospels of my Son Jesus. While many kinds of sins multiply, they are being justified as if sewage water could be claimed to be pure water. Many blind people are believing such claims. The devil, who has led them into such deceptions, is overjoyed. (November 24, 1994)

My beloved children! The Freemasons have already laid plots of darkness and are paralyzing even key activities in the Church through their followers. So, the Church should recognize my messages fast, but it is indifferent. If, as a result, even my children for whom I took great pains to rescue from the marsh fall back into the whirlpool, what will happen to them at the end of the world, and who will be responsible for that? What will be the use of regretting and beating one's chest at that time? Ah! I am sad. All the roads are becoming blocked. (June 21, 1995)

The hours of apostasy and disloyalty are afflicting you. But, if you meditate more deeply on the Lord's Sacred Heart and my Immaculate Heart, which have been torn apart, and if the messages that I give you through the little soul are spread and put into practice in the world, you will be guided through me to the high pinnacle of sanctification, offering yourselves up as living sacrifices with a heart of a martyr every day and will experience the Father's Love on the way. (October 27, 1995)

Do not place your trust in human power

Jesus: My beloved little soul! I do not forsake your praying heart. Didn't I guide Peter's small boat to safety? Do not place your trust in human power in accomplishing anything. You will suffer much amidst numerous hidden rocks and enemies' traps, but will achieve the final victory in My burning Sacred Heart. (January 26, 1993)

(One day after a major earthquake in Kobe, Japan)
Pride can ruin not only individuals but the whole world. God broke their pride with which they trusted human power, without realizing that God can destroy iron pillars and brass walls so solidly built by humans in one moment, and that He can erect them in one moment, too. But I love that country and that nation so much that, in response to the prayers of the little souls who are practicing my messages of love and following me, I will gather them under my mantle and help them be saved by returning to God, repenting their sins truthfully and living a sincere life with all their hearts. (January 18, 1995)

Numerous children are rejecting the Dogmas and causing a great disorder in the Liturgy and Laws in the Church

Numerous children, who have gone far away from my Son Jesus and me, have been swept away by storms and have fallen into errors and, because of the resulting lack of faith, are not able to accept the Dogmas and are causing a great disorder in the Liturgy and Laws in the Church. Even many shepherds have fallen into this disorder and are walking along the way to hell. The gate of hell is wide open to receive them. (February 2, 1995)

Transcend national and racial differences

(During Julia's visit to the Philippines) Yes. You have become brethren through the Lord's Precious Blood. I, your Heavenly Mother, will always be with you to help you love one another more deeply like dry land thirsting for rain. Do not worry about results, but follow me like a child. Then, I will embrace each one of you in my Immaculate Heart and bless you by pouring down fragrant oil of love upon you. (February 11, 1992)

I am Mother to all of you. Come closer to me, overcoming different nationalities and national borders. When you believe my words and follow me totally, my protection and love will be with you and great blessings by God will be bestowed upon you. (December 14, 1992)

If all my children in this world transcend national boundaries, racial barriers and factional differences, form a unity and harmony with each other, and display the power of love, the Church will be revitalized, a shining new Pentecost will be realized, and this world will be saved through the Lord, Who is present in the Eucharist. (September 24, 1994)

I am the Queen of the Universe

My beloved children! Thank you for responding joyfully to my call. Do not be concerned about how many of you are gathered here. What is important is that you become sanctified in the Lord and offer up your prayers with a sincere heart. I came down from Heaven as the Queen of the Universe enwrapped in a brilliant immaculate light in order to nurture you. (February 18, 1993)

Entrust all your difficulties to me

My beloved children! To console me and help the messages be spread and practiced, offer up your sufferings gracefully. All

Father Raymond Spies and Julia holding the Blessed Mother's statue in the Chapel in Naju. (May 27, 1993)

Pilgrims who witnessed the Eucharistic miracle in the Chapel on July 2, 1995.

the children in the world who are helping me! Entrust all your difficulties to me. Your peace should not be shaken. The devotion in a burning heart manifests itself as unlimited love and a firm and courageous determination. When you live according to the rules of love, you will not be taken over by fear, nor will your spirit be broken by despair. Now, with one ray of hope, I again ask you, whom I love. It is not too late yet. Make haste and give me a hand so that all my children who are in sins may repent. If they only repent, many sheep who are following them will obtain Heaven. (June 21, 1995)

Help those who have nothing and become their friends

Respect the dignity of humans and practice true love by helping those who have nothing instead of helping the lofty, and by finding and giving love to those who are poor, hungry and sick and becoming their friends. Prepare a place where you can welcome those who wander around and suffer; give clothes to those who have no clothes; give a warm and merciful parental care to the handicapped; and give comfort to those who have been hurt. (January 23, 1993)

Observe the Holy Hours on Thursdays

Make a constant effort to blind Satan. On Thursdays, offer reparations to the Blessed Sacrament. Pray without ceasing to constrain the evils that offend the Lord and to compensate for the sacrileges committed against the Holy Eucharist. (June 27, 1987)

I will be with you every time you gather together to observe the Holy Hours so that your prayers and sacrifices may be united with mine and offered to the Lord. You must combine your little devotions and offer them up together with mine so that they may soothe the Lord's Wounds. (February 18, 1993)

A multitude of souls are moving farther away from God and rushing toward perdition, and the whole human race is faced with an unprecedented danger to their lives and freedom. My

Son Jesus is looking down at this poor humanity, lamenting over the sinners' indifference and betrayals, and aspiring that all of you would offer the Holy Hours devotion sincerely as sacrifices and penance. (February 18, 1993)

The Holy Hours prayers that you offer compensate for the indifference, sacrileges and insults committed against the Sacred Body and Blood of Christ, Who loved the whole human race so much that He became their Food. These prayers console the pains of death He experienced at Gethsemane and the sorrows He felt because of His disciples' desertion. They also make up for numerous children's sins of violating God's Sacred Dignity and for their ingratitude and betrayals. (February 18, 1993)

The prayers, sacrifices and devotions offered for the conversion of sinners during the Holy Hours become reparations for their sins and sacrificial offerings to God's Justice. This will soften God the Father's just anger. For this reason, the Lord is pleased to accept the reparations and devotions offered during the Holy Hours. The Lord promised a plenary indulgence to those souls who make a sincere Confession, receive Holy Communion, and observe the Holy Hours well, by pouring down His Spirit into them and bathing them in His Sacred Blood. This promise will surely be kept. (February 18, 1993)

My children, whom I love so dearly! Do not try to calculate the outcome in human ways and out of curiosity. You must know that the Lord's ways are so different from human ways. Do not view anything with human eyes or think in human ways, but keep and follow the Lord's Laws faithfully. The new light of grace will be bestowed, and a Resurrection and Pentecost filled with joy will come down upon all the souls who pray in the Lord's name and observe the Holy Hours before the great storm begins, wherever they may be in the world. (February 18, 1993)

All my beloved children in the world! In this urgent time, observe the Holy Hours every Thursday well which can compensate for the sins and ingratitude that have transgressed the Solemn Dignity of God. About two years ago (*on February 18, 1993*), I already told you in detail about the Thursday Holy Hours Devotion. Put it into practice by staying awake and praying. (September 7, 1995)

Fragrant oil flowing from Our Lady's forehead. (From November 24, 1992 to October 23, 1994)

My beloved daughter! As you just saw, my enemy's red army can lose power and be turned back by the fervent prayers you offer together during the Holy Hours. Right now, God's just anger is overflowing and God the Father is about to strike (the world) with His right hand that has been raised. But, thanks to the fervent prayers by you, little souls, He is delaying the hour. Therefore, stay awake and pray more fervently. From here (Heaven), I join myself with you, as you offer up ardent and strong responses and fervent and persevering prayers in sincere love and generosity. (September 7, 1995)

Help my poor little soul (Julia)

Support and give courage to my poor little soul who has to suffer pains all the time and is hated so intensely by the devil, because she has to testify for the Lord. She is now offering up her pains in reparation for the sins in the world, while being pressed down hard by a crown of thorns and covered with wounds all over herself. Isn't she a piece of live flesh torn off the humanity? (February 16, 1994)

My dear sons and daughters! When you help her, you are helping me and consoling my Immaculate Heart. The Lord will bestow graces whenever needed. So, support her so that she may spread my messages of love all over the world courageously and completely. (February 16, 1994)

She has little knowledge of this world, because it has been taken away from her so that she may participate better in the Lord's Work of Salvation and may work in me only. She often feels helpless because of this. (February 16, 1994)

When you help my little soul well and achieve unity, I will pour down fragrant balsam on you. It is a symbol of humility, faith and reliance. Do not expect to receive from each other, but give to each other. (February 16, 1994)

The Fragrance and the Oil

Spread the fragrance of roses all over the world for the prevention of wars and for the conversion of sinners. This is truly a weapon (July 15, 1985)

I am squeezing all of myself to give you the fragrance and oil. The fragrance that I give to you is a gift from God. It means my presence, love and friendship for you. (April 8, 1993)

My beloved daughter! As I shed tears and tears of blood for the conversion of sinners for 700 days, I have given you fragrant oil for 700 days until today by squeezing all of myself with all my love, for the salvation of the children in the world, after preparing and showing the fragrant oil on my head for 400 days. But how many children have returned to my bosom so far? (October 23, 1994)

There will be the Second Pentecost

I will always stay close to the Pope, help him, protect him from dangers, and be with him in the Heavenly Garden. If my words are well accepted and practiced, the chastisement which is to fall upon all of you will turn into a Second Pentecost, and the Church will be renewed by the irresistible power of the Holy Spirit and Love. (June 27, 1993)

Depending on whether you accept my words well or reject them, the time of the Second Pentecost and Purification can be advanced or delayed. Therefore, become simple and innocent babies, listening to your Mother and rushing to her. Then, you will be saved through a new Resurrection and a new Birth, and this world will surely be saved through the Lord's Resurrection. (February 4, 1994)

When you follow me believing, trusting and relying on me, I will carry out my Plan at your side through amazing methods; God the Son, Who is my Son, will establish a Kingdom of Glory filled with Love, Peace and Joy through you; and, through Him, there will be a Resurrection and a new Pentecost in this world. (November 21, 1995)

Manifest my presence

Become simple like a child and live a consecrated life. Then, I will breathe my spirit into you so that you may be nurtured with my life and become my sons and daughters who manifest the Heavenly Mother's presence. Also, you will receive floral crowns of glory in Heaven and enjoy eternal happiness at my side. (February 16, 1994)

I am the Mediatrix of Graces and the Co-Redemptrix

Sons and daughters who have been called because you are so dearly loved! This Mother, who is the Mediatrix of Graces and the Co-Redemptrix, will transform you through the little soul whom I have chosen. So, do not fear but settle down. Today, this Mother in Heaven is accepting your little hearts into my Immaculate Heart. Bravely become apostles of my Immaculate Heart in unity so that my Plan may be realized well. When you follow me walking a little person's way of love with humility, faith, reliance and trust, I will enwrap you with the armor of the Holy Spirit so that even the arrows of fire that the devil throws at you may not dare hurt you. (May 9, 1995)

Heaven rejoices when even one more sinner repents

I did not come to call the just. Because the sinners are walking on the road to hell, I wanted you to work with me to save even one more soul. (July 15, 1987)

My beloved daughter! How could I be unaware of your agonizing heart? Do not be troubled. Do not cry. What the Lord and this Mother want is that even one more sinner who has been lost repents. When a sinner repents, God the Father, God the Son and God the Holy Spirit, together with all of God's Saints and angels in Heaven, will rejoice. Doesn't the Bible tell you about a father throwing a big banquet when one of his sons, who had been lost, returned? (June 19, 1995)

Prepare a book of testimonies

Do your best in everything and prepare a book with testimonies from many children who have received love from the Lord through me so that you may not fall into the grave events filled with pains. If they give testimony on the graces they have received, they will receive more blessings. How would it be possible that many people receive graces except through pains? Why are you hesitating and trying to give it up? Execute it without reservation. Do you understand this? The current age demands miracles. That is why I prepared a plan. Why are you trying to give it up with your own thinking? Do not follow the wishes of the enemies, but obey this Mother's words in a simple way. (June 11, 1995)

Numerous people are spiritually blind and deaf and are rejecting my presence, because their hearts are so dried up in extreme poverty and lack of understanding. That is why I am asking your spiritual director and you to publish a book with testimonies on the graces that many children have received. Do not worry about the consequences, but march ahead bravely. (June 11, 1995)

This Heavenly Mother will take care of the results and accomplish amazing fruits. Those who are walking the way of ruin and destruction, judging and criticizing (me), will come back as simple and good children following this Mother, thanks to the book. Some of those who are distancing me now may still refuse to accept me. A day will come when they will beat their chests for shame. Make haste. I am asking you, because I want to protect the numerous children who are walking toward hell. Stay alert remembering that my enemy is active, violent and dangerous and is trying to topple you. (June 11, 1995)

Let's compare this to a gold coin. If the gold coin is wrapped and stored, it will be of no use. Likewise, precious writings will be of no use, unless they are made known. Those who have ears will hear and follow this Mother. Make them known in a hurry. Then, you will harvest richly and numerous sheep will return to the Bosom of the Lord. Listen well. Those who give to others will receive more, and those who hide (what they have) from others will be deprived of what they have. Who can possibly obstruct God's Will? Do not hesitate, as the time left is short. Also, I am the one who is doing the work. (June 19, 1995)

This book that I want will richly fill the hearts of the arid souls. And, because of this book, the practice of the messages will multiply. It will be a precious gift that will help open people's closed hearts and make them seek me. Therefore, do not worry, but comply with the wishes of this Mother who is undergoing a death agony. God has sent angels to His servants in order to show them what is about to happen. Now, do not delay, but hurry up. I will guard and protect you. What will be written in that book are fruits and living testimonies. Those who walk in the daytime do not fall, because there is light. But those who walk at night can fall easily, because there is no light. (June 19, 1995)

Do not approach me out of curiosity or as spectators

I am asking you, because there are many children who come here for curiosity and are seeking miracles and signs. Offer more sacrifices and reparations so that all the children, upon hearing my eager voice of love, may live the messages actively and follow me with confidence. Bring them to me, and, when they follow me completely, I will embrace them with love and let them receive the heavenly joy. (June 30, 1990)

All my children! Do not approach me because of curiosity and as spectators, but follow me with complete trust. You may not fully understand my words now, but will some day. If you refuse to believe and follow my words, however, you will surely regret it. (June 30, 1995)

Time is urgent

My dear children! In this age, so many children are being enveloped in a huge storm, while walking toward their perdition. Now is the precious time for your repentance. Do not ignore, but accept well my earnest appeals that I send to you in many different ways, while you are in the middle of an extreme danger. Even among the children I love so dearly, only a very few respond to my call in a genuine way. (January 21, 1994)

Now is the best opportunity for you to repent. When God sends a warning, sufferings accompany, too. But if you repent and comply with my requests, the cup of God's blessings will be bestowed upon you. So, do not waste this precious time and opportunity. I have already indicated several times through Fr. Gobbi and you, who *(Julia)* is unworthy, that this current age is extremely urgent. (January 18, 1995)

You must not waste any precious time, in order to prevent everyone from destruction. Do not be discouraged, but make haste to quench the Lord's thirst. (June 18, 1995)

The decisive time that can determine the fate of the whole human race is being prepared. Therefore, hurriedly wake up from sleep and listen to the voice of this Heavenly Mother who is imploring you so ardently. (September 7, 1995)

Jesus is returning to you through my Immaculate Heart

The darkness is even infiltrating the Church in coldhearted and elaborate ways. Thus, the last hour of bleeding for purification is waiting for you. If you do not live according to the Words of Truth, you will soon suffer calamities and will surely regret it. What is the use of regretting after the justice of God is realized? I am imploring like this to my children, as the time permitted for conversion is approaching its end. Be awake and pray without procrastinating. Also become simple like a child. Nobody knows the exact time of the Lord's coming to you. Preparations are in progress to defeat His enemies, destroy them and establish His Kingdom on earth. Prepare to greet Him with trust, love and faith. He is coming to you through me, your Mother. As He was sent to you by God the Father through my virgin body, Jesus will return to you through my Immaculate Heart as the King. (January 29, 1991)

Pray and pray fervently

Combine your forces. Pray without ceasing for the souls that are not turning away from the road that leads to their perdition. (September 15, 1985)

You must pray together constantly for world peace and the conversion of sinners. (January 29, 1989)

The numerous souls who have brought about an imbalance in the universe because of their excessive pride will convert and world peace will be achieved through my fervent calls and tears and through the prayers, sacrifices and reparations by the little souls. (November 26, 1989)

Hurriedly pray and pray. As the Apostles gathered and prayed together with me in the Cenacle in Jerusalem in preparation for the Descent of the Holy Spirit, you, too, should pray with me in my Immaculate Heart as the Apostles of these end times. (November 21, 1995)

Dear children who have been called by me! Pray with a greater sincerity and with love. Through the prayers that you offer together tonight, which has been set aside (for you) to be with me, the devil, who is afflicting you and is causing confusion through deceptions so that even the children who have been called by me may become alienated from my love, can be repelled. (January 6, 1996)

APPENDIX

Marian Era: from 1830
Marian apparitions, manifestations, and ecclesiastical events:

1830 The Miraculous Medal apparition in Paris (France)

1836 Our Lady of Victories Church, Archconfrat. of the Immaculate Heart of Mary in Paris (France)

1840 The Green Badge/Scapular of the Immaculate Heart of Mary in Blangy (France)

1842 St. Louis de Montfort's book *True Devotion to the Blessed Virgin Mary* is found in Saint Laurent-sur-Sevre (France)

1846 Apparition of Our Lady of LaSalette (France)

1854 Dogma of the Immaculate Conception declared by Pope Pius IX (Rome)

1858 Apparition of the Immaculate Conception at Lourdes (France)

1871 Apparition of Our Lady at Pontmain (France)

1875–6 Our Lady of Pompeii, Confraternity of Queen of the Holy Rosary, connected with Bl. Bartolo Longo (Italy)

1876 Apparition at Pellevoisin (France)

1879 Apparition at Knock (Ireland)

1883 Establishing Shrine of Our Lady of the Cape: Queen of the Holy Rosary (Canada)

1895 First National Marian Congress at Livorno (Italy)

1900 First International Marian Congress at Lyons (France) (The first of at least sixteen such Congresses regularly held all over the world down to our own day)

1906 Our Lady of Sorrows; miraculous painting at Quito (Ecuador)

1917 Our Lady of the Rosary appears at Fatima (Portugal)

1921	The Legion of Mary was founded (Ireland)
1932	The Immaculate Heart of Mary appears at Beauraing (Belgium)
1933	Apparition at Banneux (Belgium)
1942	Consecration of the world to the Immaculate Heart of Mary, (1st) by Pope Pius XII on October 31 (Rome)
1946	Apparition at Marienfried (Germany)
1950	Assumption of the Blessed Virgin Mary: dogma defined by Pope Pius XII (Rome)
1952	Consecration of the world to the Immaculate Heart of Mary, (2nd), Pope Pius XII on July 7
1953	Weeping Image of the Immaculate Heart of Mary (August 29-September 1) at Syracuse, Sicily (Italy)
1954	Marian Year, (1st), decreed by Pope Pius XII in *Fulgens Corona"* (September 8, 1953)
1954	Proclamation of Queenship of Mary in *Ad Coeli Reginam* by Pius XII (October 11)
1964	Consecration of the world to the Immaculate Heart of Mary (3rd), by Pope Paul VI, November 21, during the II Vatican Council
1964	Mary declared "Mother of the Church" by Pope Paul VI on November 21 at II Vatican Council
1964	Victory of Our Lady of the Holy Rosary (Brazil)
1967	*The Great Sign* on the 50th anniversary of Fatima, by Pope Paul VI (May 13)
1972	Marian Movement of Priests founded at Milan (Italy)
1972	Our Lady appears at Akita (Japan)
1974	*Marialis Cultus* by Pope Paul VI on devotion to the Blessed Virgin Mary (February 2)
1982	Consecration of the world to the Immaculate Heart, (4th), by Pope John Paul II on May 13
1984	Consecration of the world to the Immaculate Heart of Mary, (5th), renewed by Pope John Paul II on March 25, together with the Bishops of the world
1985	Our Lady manifests herself at Naju (Korea)
198	—Marian Year (2nd) (June 1987 till August 15, 1988) decreed by Pope John Paul II in *Mother of the Redeemer* (March 25)

Information on ordering more copies of this book:
Our Lady's Messages from Naju—
Compiled according to subject

Copies	Price per copy	S&H charge	Total price
1	$5.95	$2.00	$7.95
5	5.00	4.00	29.00
10	4.50	6.00	49.00
25	4.00	9.00	109.00
50	3.50	14.00	189.00

(The above prices apply to shipments within the U.S.A.)

Send orders to: **Mary's Touch By Mail**
P.O. Box 1668
Gresham, OR 97030
Phone: (503) 669-8443
VISA & MasterCard also accepted

Other materials available

1. Book: *Messages of Love—The Mother of the Savior Speaks to the World from Naju, Korea*
All the messages that Julia Kim in Naju, Korea, received from Our Lord and Our Lady between July 1985 and January 1996, plus Julia's narrations describing the circumstances surrounding the messages. 304 pages including about 60 photos (B&W). This book replaces the previous book titled: *The Miracle in Naju, Korea.*
   Price: $12.95 plus $3.00 S&H

2. Video: *Mary Draws Us To The Eucharist*
A summary of the Church teachings on the Holy Eucharist and the video footages and photos taken during the Eucharistic miracles through Julia Kim in Naju, Korea between June 1988 and July 1995. Includes the seventh Eucharistic miracle that occurred during the Apostolic Pro Nuncio's visit on November 24, 1994 and the miracle of seven Sacred Hosts on July 1, 1995. Music by the Pontifical Choir of Kansas City. VHS, 68 min.
   Price: $15.95 plus $2.00 S&H

3. Video: *The Queen of the Holy Rosary in Naju, Korea*
A comprehensive summary of the supernatural signs and messages in Naju since their beginning in 1985. Scenes of the Blessed Mother's statue weeping tears and tears of blood; the same statue exuding fragrant oil; Julia suffering the pains of the Crucifixion and abortion; Eucharistic miracles and more. This video is recommended as a general introduction to Naju. VHS, 55 min.
   Price: $14.95 plus $2.00 S&H

Send orders to: **Mary's Touch By Mail**
P.O. Box 1668, Gresham, OR 97030
Phone: (503) 669-8443
VISA & MasterCard also accepted